Re-Membering:

Putting Mind and Body Back Together
Following Traumatic Brain Injury

By,

Ann Millett-Gallant

ISBN-13: 978-1490524733
ISBN-10: 1490524738

Table of Contents

All images may be viewed in color at:
www.facebook.com/remembering.millett.gallant

•

Lost. And Found?

For much of 2007, my existence may best be characterized as lost. I lost weight, lost hair, lost part of my skull, lost much muscular movement and fluidity, and lost my mobility. I lost my memory, my history, my savings, my sense of security, and my identity. I had lost my mind.

Backing up – In May of 2007, I was vacationing in San Francisco with my friend, Anna. We were exiting a café, and for some unknown reason, I shot ahead on my travel scooter and fell off the high curb of the sidewalk into the street. According to Anna, I was not obviously drunk, sick, excessively tired, or otherwise impaired before this. It was unexplainable. I hit my head, began to bleed, and an ambulance was called.

This was all told to me later, as I have no recollection of the accident, any of the trip, or even planning it. I have blocked the whole experience out. I have blocked a lot of experiences out. Even as my memory congeals, much of my life takes place in stories and photographs, but not in the sensations of BEING there. I don't have any flashes of being in the San Francisco hospital for six weeks after part of my skull was removed to allow for swelling, much of the time in a coma. I recall very little of my time spent in a rehab hospital in Columbus, OH (where I grew up and my family lives). I only remember grueling therapy sessions there and one kind nurse, who let me have the whole container of chocolate pudding that was used to help me swallow medications. I moved in with my mother at the end of the summer, in a place she had rented, which I thought was her home I didn't remember. Slowly, my strength and endurance came back. I exercised, read, wrote in a journal, drew in a sketchbook, and began to re-member – to put mind and body back together. Yet, I was content to rarely leave my sanctuary.

In a couple months, I had surgery on my skull to reconstruct it, after which, I had been told, I would improve drastically. Unfortunately, I had to endure a week in the hospital before I had the surgery, after an anesthesiologist punctured my lungs trying to put an IV in my chest. But I digress. I did feel better after my skull was intact, and in just a few weeks, I began teaching an online class, one of the three that I was supposed to be teaching full time that Fall. My knowledge of art history, the humanities, and how to teach came right back and, likely, got stronger. I was able to better concentrate and exert more authority over time. I soon moved back to my home in North Carolina and to my boyfriend, whose name I could now remember. As 2008 progressed, so did I, and I was determined to no longer put anything off. I proposed to the man I love and got married,

6

taught full time, and began to write scholarly articles and to paint again. But I was still lost.

Backing up further – As a congenital amputee, I have been physically disabled since birth. I was born asymmetrical, as my right extremities are longer than my left; my right arm ends with a pointy tip, which serves as my hand; and my left arm ends just below the elbow with a soft, tiny finger known as a "residual limb." My right leg ends below the knee with another residual limb I have called my "tickle" since I was a child, and my left leg is a few inches long and appears like a ball with a large dimple at the end. My physique is illustrated throughout this book and especially in images from chapters 1 and 3. Indoors, I crawl or move around on the floor in a seated position, in an act I call my "butt scoot," and I use prosthetic legs and crutches to walk some. I learned how to manipulate my finger-free hands and legs with numerous adaptations, such that I can do almost anything I want to do with practice, innovation, and the right resources. I have also incorporated disability studies as a discipline, as well as my identity as a disabled woman, into my teaching and writing. I am (was?) independent and proud of it. I have traveled internationally, lived in three cities, and gotten my PhD. I was, for better or worse, fearless.

Now I feel anxious taking my scooter to the grocery store. But the anxiety about injury lessens over time. The anxiety over being lost and having lost control are still, and may always be, unbearable. I can't sleep through the night, my moods fluctuate from high to low without warning, and I can't remember certain people, places, and personal things. I sometimes have to laugh as I realize that not everyone looks oddly familiar because I have forgotten them, but because people just look alike. I can laugh at my loss, at times, while at other times I am consumed by feelings of emptiness and the desire to know what happened, and why.

I have learned countless things from my accident, about myself and the world I live in. But the main thing I have learned is that "lost" and "found" are not absolutes. They are states of being, always in flux. They collide, overlap, and intertwine. Sometimes, they make it a chore to get up in the morning. And sometimes, they produce accidental masterpieces.

I draw the term "accidental masterpiece" from a volume of essays by *The New York Times* art critic and columnist Michael Kimmelman (2005). The readings explore the many intersections between art and everyday life, with the theme that art is the ultimate accident. Accidents in literal and figurative forms catalyze discovery, insight, creative production, and indeed, often "accidental" (unexpected and fortuitous) masterpieces. I center one of my courses on this text, and the students have a writing assignment based on tales of loss and discovery. I was inspired by the course to write the beginning of this book.

I created one of many accidental masterpieces in the form of a collage, which predates this book and reflects many themes of my experiences during my accident and recovery. The title of the collage, *Re-Membering*, refers to the ongoing process of integrating the past with present, as well as synthesizing my mental, emotional, and corporeal transformations. It is featured on the cover of this book. The collage format embodies my accident and recovery both visually and viscerally; these visual fragments "collide, overlap, and intertwine," as do my states of mind. I describe my memory as a random collage of stories and pictures that are not contained by an overarching narrative. It is both a jumble and a medley. Like my thought patterns and my memory, the collage is composed of images, words, and objects that do not illustrate a linear narrative, but rather relate piece by piece, in a chain of associations. Framing the canvas is a selection of get well cards, chosen from a countless stack, which shows the range of people who thought of and reached out to me. Indeed, the support of friends and family got me through my ordeals. The cards strategically range from sentimental to humorous and arrived from close relatives, as well as distant acquaintances. Visually, this frame juxtaposes elephants and kittens, a cartoon image of Dr. Phil, a crayon-drawn "You Go Girl" card, designed by my five and three year old nieces, fields with soaring clouds, gilded lily pads, and magical fairies.

Within the frame are photographs of me in a coma from the San Francisco hospital, as well as business cards and prescriptions from my doctors. These medical images are juxtaposed with more happy photographs, especially of my wedding, which was my symbol of moving on and celebrating my life. At the rehearsal dinner, my father presented to me a drawing of my imagined wedding, created by me as a child, a copy of which stands amongst the photographs of that reality in the collage. There are also sketches that I made from magazine pictures and drawings I later created on top of printed photographs when I existed in "my own private world" and the idea of creating a new, original drawing seemed overwhelming. In one such example, I sketched in pink pen over a printed photograph I took of my prosthetic feet at the beach. I call this photograph "There's No Place Like the Beach," with reference to the Wizard of Oz (because of my Dorothy-esque sparkling red shoes). The placement of this image in the collage recalls the wounded and bleeding feet in Frida Kahlo's surrealistic self-portrait *What the Water Gave Me,* (1938), in which fragmented images from her memory, history, and fantasy assemble and float in the water surrounding her body. Frida Kahlo was impaired by a bus accident at the age of eighteen and became a disabled artist who made brilliant, passionate paintings of her colorful life and many body experiences. Kahlo has always been my favorite artist - my idol of sorts - and now I find yet another connection to her because of my accident. I also placed in my collage a photograph of me as a child in a gymnastics class. I pose exuberantly, with a huge smile on my face and my arms extended in the air, as I model a colorful leotard that frames my short legs. I included this image because I remember how early in life, I was very active and encouraged to be so by my doctors; physical activity was a form of therapy for me. I now work with a physical therapist, Abby, who has become a friend and a personal trainer of sorts. The prescription on my collage is for physical therapy, and the inclusion of visually disparate, yet contextually related images exemplifies a number of such juxtapositions in the collage. Additional body images include "finger paintings" of my hands, which I smeared on the canvas. One red hand sits on the edge of a page from my journal, in which I typed out Elizabeth Bishop's poem "Insomnia." My many sleepless nights now bring new meaning for me to an old favorite.

Although the collage is hardly a masterpiece in the conventional sense, it is an expression of my inner strength. I put energy and frustration and confusion into it. It composes a lot of raw, imperfect, random, and impulsive feelings. In this way, it is therapeutic. This book is like a collage. It is decidedly nonlinear, never two-dimensional, and composed of fragments of text and images. This is a story of highs and lows, triumphs and failures, and hope and disillusionment. Each chapter/essay is composed of personal narrative, research on brain injury and art therapy, information from my medical records, and voices from other relevant memoirs. I also engage the perspectives of my physical therapist, my art therapist, my brain surgeon, and my husband and family as I describe the therapeutic processes of my recovery in all its dimensions.

Chapter 1, "Falling Together," combines medical information and personal details about my accident and rehabilitation. I focus on the vital roles of my family and friends in my recovery, my strengthened and sometimes strained relationships with them, and the effects my accident had on their relationships with each other. I also stress the importance of hope and support. Chapter 2, "Brain Injury Moments" discusses the cognitive implications of my injury and how it affected my memory and emotions and how it increased my anxiety. I engage here both personal narrative and research on brain injury. In chapter 3, "A Leg to Stand On," I turn to the physical and anatomical effects of my accident, specifically, issues I had with muscle contraction and dysfunction of my knee, and my work with my physical therapist and now friend, Abby. I also discuss in this chapter my battles with prosthetic legs and my changes in identity with and without them, as well as my transforming body image. These first three chapters are all illustrated with examples of my artwork, and in chapter 4, "Art Therapy and Collage," I focus on my experiences with art therapy. I provide a brief introduction to the theories behind and history of art therapy as a practice and discuss in more detail my own art therapy practices. I also focus on the media of collage as a therapeutic practice and as a revolutionary art form. Finally, in my Conclusion, "Forgiveness," I summarize the negative and positive effects these experiences have had on my life and explain how and why I wrote this book.

Falling Together

I believe there are many tools on the road to recovery
– family above all, exercise, music, and even the
reassurance of touch.
  -    Lee Woodruff (2009, 275)

My family and friends fostered my recovery after the accident, and while relationships that were established before my accident deepened, new friendships also formed. My friend and travel companion Anna got on the phone just after the ambulance took me to the hospital in San Francisco and began a long chain of communications throughout my support system. She first called Paul, my boyfriend with whom I lived, but got no answer. She then called my step-sister and best friend, Brandee, who also lives in Durham, NC, who then called my father with the news. He got a hold of my Mom, who immediately packed and booked a flight to San Francisco. I can't imagine her state when she arrived there, and she admits that for the next month or so, she often felt in a daze. "Luckily" (so I am told), my accident happened quite close to a premiere trauma center, San Francisco General Hospital, to which I was taken immediately. I would learn later that I entered the emergency room alert, although

I had been unconscious for ten minutes, I had a blown pupil, and doctors said that I was within twenty minutes of dying.

I don't remember anything about being in San Francisco. Medical records state that during my time there, I experienced a urinary tract infection, intermittent hypertension, and a pneumonia likely caused by my ventilator. I was also on medication for a peptic ulcer. These records list so many details about the levels of every gas and vitamins in my blood. Every organ was evaluated, and ultrasounds were performed. I must have been looked at all over through a microscope. The records also describe how a 17 gauge feeding tube was inserted into my abdomen. I remained in the intensive care unit until June 19, 2007.

In the San Francisco hospital, I was unconscious a lot of the time, and when I was awake, my mom told me, I was very agitated and even had painful muscle spasms. I know she spent a lot of time with me, talking to and massaging me. I also think she helped with grooming, by plucking my eyebrows. She was quite literally hands on! Annoyed that I was having trouble swallowing and that the nurses weren't doing anything about it, she one day closed my door, stuck her fingers down my throat, and cleared out a "hunk of junk." After that, I swallowed fine. Mother knows best!

While much of what I have heard about my time in San Francisco is heart-wrenching, there are these stories that make me smile. For example, Brandee told me later that I had a very hot physical therapist (tall, athletic, and handsome), and one day, he climbed into bed with me and began to thrust me back and forth across the bed to practice my falling reflexes. Brandee tried to duplicate the look I had on my face that she found so amusing, which made me think that I didn't know what was going on and whether or not to enjoy it. She also said – at the time – she and my Dad were uncomfortably amused. I'm glad to hear that there was comic relief! Brandee also told me of times she shared a hotel room with my Dad while I was in the hospital and commented, "He was in a lot of pain."

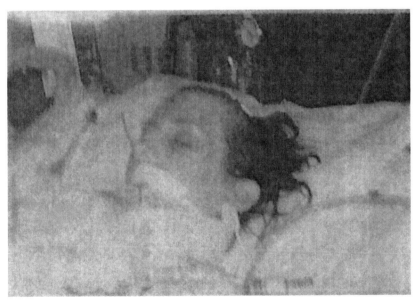

Fig. 1: Photograph of Ann Millett-Gallant in the San Francisco General Hospital, May/June 2007

I believe my Mom took the photographs I have of me in the hospital, hooked up to devices by tubes, with my eyes closed and no semblance of consciousness on my face (fig. 1). In medical terms, I had a subdural hematoma of 1.8 cm in size, and I received a right hemicraniectomy (removal of skull bones) and a medically-induced coma to allow my brain the space and time to swell. My surgical notes report that I didn't respond to any stimulus following surgery, so physical and occupation therapy were put on hold. Then, on July 1, my mental status improved drastically. I began to respond to stimuli and commands and seemed to recognize my name. I knew I lived in North Carolina, but for some reason thought it was the 1980s. For the next few days, I didn't maintain much awareness, and my doctors thought I might need more release from pressure in my brain. By July 10, I was alert and responsive again. By July 22, I was responding to jokes, but it wasn't until August 3 that I began to talk, recall names, and to be aware of my location. Continuous progress reports note increases in the number of my platelets and more neurological activity, as I was slowly weaned off ventilation. My catheter was finally removed, although I then had to wear diapers. My medical team watched my fluid collection, inflammation, and increases in blood pressure and temperature, as my loved ones watched for my recognition of their presence. In these photographs, you can see hints that my skull looks like it has collapsed in on one side, however, this indentation was not yet as drastic as it would become once the swelling decreased.

My Mom and other visitors faced this appearance of me, trying to remain optimistic as they waited for me to wake up and breathe on my own. My Mom has also said that I was pretty nonresponsive (I was, after all, in a coma), but that the first time I seemed animated was when Paul came to visit. She said he walked in the room, and my eyes widened as I stared at him. She could tell I was very happy to see him. Mom says Paul cried at my bedside and told me repeatedly that he loved me. That's sweet, even if for weeks after, I still called him "Matt," the name of my ex-boyfriend. I believe it was the names I had confused, not the people. I have also heard about how Paul slept on the couch in my Mom's hotel room one night, which was awkward for both of them. I have heard stories from my mom about the city, and how she and Paul liked to explore. Mom said it was unexpectedly chilly in San Francisco in May, and she had to buy warmer clothes, so they went to an awesome two-story Target! They both knew and talked about how much I would have loved that, as an avid Target fan. A last story I've been told was that my Mom was trying to help me learn to handle objects, by having me hold a spoon, when I looked at her and said, "Mom, this is really dumb." Despite that the doctors predicted I wouldn't drive a car again, may not be able to teach, and, worst case scenario, would be in a vegetative state, she said she knew then that I would get better.

As represented in my "Re-Membering" collage, the stories of my accident and recovery exist in written, visual, and often distorted fragments. My Mom has expressed that she wishes she remembered more details and had written things down, but she suffered her own trauma. I know my Dad and stepmother, Sherry; my step-sister, Brandee, and her husband, Jamie; and especially Paul, visited me in San Francisco. My stepmother's sister, Peggy, was a nurse in California and came to see me and to translate my condition to my other visitors. My sister, Jennie, also traveled to San Francisco, providing support and help in documenting my healing. My sister and I have always been friendly, but never very close. We have different interests, needs, and life plans, yet rereading her journals from San Francisco made me realize we share the need to write. It also made me see how much love she has for me. I was both touched and sad when I later read the journal she kept, especially this entry:

- unlikely that she'll recover to level that she was before
- infection may cause seizure

Overall, impression from <u>long</u> talk w/Dr. Stivers and Twyla:
She wants to make sure how ???? the situation was/is. Maybe so we realize we're in for a long haul? Almost like she wants us to be informed & prepared for the worst.
She did say several times she has a good feeling though. And she's admitted Annie's made progress,

esp. because lots of emer. rooms wouldn't even have operated. She was about 20 min. from dying.
I told her we were taking this all 1 day at a time, one step at a time in this marathon

Dear Annie –
<u>Please</u> wake up. <u>Please</u>.

I am both touched and disturbed by these sentiments. I am thankful and honored by all the love and support that surrounded me, and I am proud to have fostered new-found respect and relationships between my family members and friends. I also feel sad to think about how much pain my accident caused for so many of them.

I've also heard about what was called my "great escape" from San Francisco. The people at San Francisco General Hospital suggested I transfer to a rehab hospital nearby, and Paul even offered to move to San Francisco to be close to me. I received excellent care there, but my loved ones wanted me closer to home. Apparently, they tried to get me into a hospital in Durham, but I wasn't accepted because I didn't have insurance. I had been using the Cobra program to extend my graduate school insurance, and it had run out just a couple of months before I was to start a new fulltime job at the University of North Carolina at Greensboro. I always assumed I ended up in Columbus because my parents wanted me closer to them. But I also went to Columbus because we already had medical connections there, like Ernie

Johnson, who was my physical medicine and rehabilitation doctor from when I was a child and who was on the board of Dodd Hall, the rehabilitation hospital of The Ohio State University in Columbus. When my Mom first called Dr. Johnson with the news, and I'm sure it was in panic and tears, he immediately told her that I was strong, and that I would be fine. I know it was a great comfort to her. He told me later that when he heard from my mother that I was injured and they didn't know where I should go, he simply said, "Put her on a plane." I flew from San Francisco to Cincinnati with my Mom and my sister, Jennie, in first class. My Dad met us to take Jennie back to Columbus, while a medical van drove me and Mom to Dodd Hall at the OSU medical center.

There was still a long road ahead. My medical records report that when I arrived at Dodd Hall, I was alert, but I was emaciated and had poor lung function, coarse breathing, double vision and extreme hypertension. Despite these complications, Dr. Johnson says that when he first came to see me, I opened my eyes and said, "Hi, Ernie." My only flashes of memory from when I was in Dodd Hall were lying in a bed and being brought my medications each day. A spoonful of chocolate pudding was used to help get me to swallow them, and I requested to have the whole container. I do love chocolate. I also know from my records that I struggled with muscle spasticity and increased tone, for which I was prescribed Dantrium and had several Botox injections in my right hip, knee, and arm. I was also taking Ritalin for stimulation, because I was still somewhat comatose.

In early August, my blood pressure rose again to 150s/90s, my heart rate increased to 150s, and I had extreme pain in my right leg, for which I was given more Damtrium, Vicodin, and Valium. I was transferred to the emergency room. My vitals were stable when I arrived there, but it was recommended that the Ritalin be stopped and Dantrium reduced. At the time of discharge from Dodd Hall, my long list of medications included: Tylenol for headaches and Lortrab for pain; Dulculax (a laxative) and Colace (a stool softener), for constipation; Celexa for anxiety and depression; Dantrium for muscle spasms; and Ambien for sleep.

The accident affected me deeply, of course, but also it impacted everyone surrounding me, and in many cases, brought them closer. Emails about my progress were sent out from my Mom and from Brandee to all my friends in North Carolina. These emails were then forwarded to the listserv of the Art Department at UNC Chapel Hill, were I had done my PhD work. My supportive community extended broadly and responded with encouragement and support. The emails from my mom in San Francisco serve as a chronicle of my steady improvements there: Ann's breathing tube was removed, her temperature lowered, Ann answered yes and no questions today, Ann made eye contact today, Ann recognized and responded to Paul, Ann's address is:, Ann got in front of a laptop today. Later emails reported that my spirits were mostly high, although I had painful muscle spasms and a great deal of memory loss. A particular email that stands out for me was from Brandee, dated Thursday Aug 9:

> Hi everybody - I thought you might like to hear that Ann was released from
> Dodd Hall today to live in her new digs in Columbus! She will be staying
> with her mom in an apartment while she continues going in a couple days a
> week for rehab. She wants to get back to work in October - let's keep our
> fingers crossed! She has kept her sense of humor during her time in
> "prison" (that's her word for the hospital) and made huge progress in her
> speech and mobility. Also she apparently is famous, featured on the front
> page of the Columbus Dispatch today (you can look for the article at
> www.dispatch.com) Leave it to Ann!
>
> I'll be going up to Columbus on Saturday for a few days. She is thirsty for
> news and glad to hear about her good friends. I'm glad to convey any
> messages or items up there, or if you want you can try and reach her by
> phone. She does have some hiccups in her short-term memory, especially
> recent developments (I guess that's sort of obvious!) I'm really looking
> forward to seeing her after so long. -Brandee

I love how this email conveys that my personality and idiosyncrasies were emerging and were good signs for my family. The email also reflects my relationship with Brandee. The Columbus Dispatch article she refers to is titled "Willpower" and featured a photograph of me wearing mascara and showing how my head on my right side was concave, after my swelling had gone down. The reporter stated that a section of my skull the size of a grapefruit was removed. I made a self-portrait sketch from the image, which resembles, but does not exactly duplicate the original (fig. 2). What struck me when I first viewed the newspaper image was my concave head, yet as I looked at it again and again, and studied it in more detail in order to draw it, my eyes looked back at me. My sketch emphasizes the eyes in size and marks because they reflect my own humanity. In the original photograph, I look like a deer caught in the headlights; upon additional views, these eyes reveal to me my own determination. The photograph is still shocking for me to look at, and I always wince when I think about how I must have looked to strangers, and even more dramatically, to those who loved me. This article and these emails are pieces of the collage that are my recorded history.

Fig. 2: *Self-Portrait with Hemicraniectomy*, 2011

Despite being still somewhat heavily medicated, I made great progress before I left Dodd Hall at the end of August to stay with my Mother. The doctors there were excellent, and I had constant visitors. If I had been in North Carolina, Paul wouldn't have been able to visit me every day, and he definitely couldn't have taken care of me full time after my release from the hospital. My Mom took time off work and stayed home with me. She lifted me in and out of chairs, into bed, where I surrounded myself with comforting stuffed animals, and onto the toilet, which had a special seat over it with arm rests to grasp. It was a challenge, yet I was grateful that I no longer had to wear diapers. She cooked for me, took me places, and invited people over. She got movies and television shows on DVD, such as "Entourage," for us to watch. I remember later reading novels and writing in a journal. Writing was frustrating for me, as I express in the journal in complaints and scratchy writing. I didn't write much of substance.

These personal processes of rehabilitation were supplemented by professionals. My discharge records from Dodd Hall report that I had more work to do on eating, toileting, and transfers (on and off toilet, in and out of bed) and that I should continue core strengthening and practicing with my prostheses, but that I was already reached my discharge goals in areas of Communication and Cognition. In fact, I had already surpassed the goals for "Expression." This makes me smile. Once I was an out-patient and living at home, the only place I really had to go to in Columbus was therapy. I enjoyed and loathed it. I would get "dressed up," as much as possible: I wore makeup and color coordinated everything, even my underwear. I still like to color coordinate my underwear, because it makes me feel more together. After primping myself, my Mom would drive me to the hospital, where we would get valet parking. It felt like such a luxury.

I had speech, occupational, and physical therapy, all of which I remember vaguely and to varying degrees. Numerous reports from my medical records have helped me chart my actions and progression in these therapies, yet memories mainly reveal my feeling towards them. I disliked speech therapy. I can't remember exactly why, but I do remember it seemed mostly about swallowing and not very productive. Difficulty with swallowing is a common effect of brain injury, but my swallowing improved over time and largely due to my own practice. I can't recall occupational therapy at all, yet my records report that I practiced skills for dressing, eating, and washing my face, and performed exercises to straighten my right arm. I do recall the splint I wore at night on my arm, which disrupted my already troubled sleep and often put me into tears. My prior experience with occupational therapy was in elementary school, much of which was writing and art projects, but I don't sense my occupational therapy at Dodd Hall was as much fun. Physical therapy was exhausting, although I liked exercising, and it sometimes felt like I had a personal trainer.

Because I had hit the left side of my head, the whole right side of my body was paralyzed at first, and I regained mobility inconsistently. I remember doing exercises often in PT to try to get my knee to bend, which were frustrating and painful. I had to wear the painful splint at night on my right arm, because it was stuck to my side with a 90 degree angle. I looked, and felt, really tight and immobile. My knee was in full extension, until I gradually forced it to bend a little bit, but not enough to be very functional. I eventually began trying to walk on my prostheses. They didn't fit, because I had lost weight (especially a lot of muscle), so I had to wear a helmet and a "gate belt," which was essentially a leash, as I was lead in circles around the PT rooms at the clinic. I was always worn out, physically and emotionally, after my therapy sessions. But I was diligent about following all the techniques and programs, because I have always been a hard-working student, but also because I knew I was getting stronger.

I remember one of the only ways to get me out of the house, other than my required therapy, was with the temptation of shopping. Retail therapy! I didn't go out much before I had my skull reconstruction. I had a really big chunk removed from my skull and had to wear an institutional-looking helmet whenever I went outside of my home. As a visibly disabled person, I am used to stares to some degree, but I imagine I would have received horrified ones. My Mom and I would also see movies. All I had to do was sit in the dark. Other than that, I remember not wanting to go out much. One afternoon when my good friend, Ellen, was visiting, my mom talked us into going out for dinner. This is one example of how she was often pushy, and in this instance, I appreciated it. The dinner out was nice, although I felt really awkward the whole time. It felt forced, and I didn't want to be in such a sea of people. I was, in many ways, socially awkward. Yet the individual relationships I had with a few trusted friends and family members intensified.

Mom and I already had a close relationship, but it got even stronger. I often resented her constant caretaking attitude with me (before the accident, because of my fiercely independent spirit), but after my accident, I took great comfort in how easy it was to let her feed me, bathe me, and tuck me in. I welcomed the feeling of protection and love I felt as a child. Yet, I mostly admire her for not making me feel like a child. She treated me with respect. She let me make decisions and did not coddle me. I think she played a key role in my recovery. She was very encouraging, stayed positive, and never made me feel like I was dependent on her.

I have always had s strong relationship with my Dad, however, after my accident, it was increasingly strained. I could tell he didn't treat me the same, or perhaps, my state made him so upset that he couldn't relate to me. He expressed his feelings best through anger, which I believe is more common with men. He wanted to sue the scooter company, was distrustful of the doctors in San Francisco, and called Anna several times to rehash everything we had done that day and to ask, specifically, if I was drunk. He has asked me these questions since then and always hits a nerve, as he fans the flames of the inferno that is my guilt. He would also lecture me when I was in Columbus about my job and how I needed to call Bob (Hansen, my supervisor at UNCG, who talked with my Dad on the phone after my accident). I remember one day he came over to the place I lived with my Mom (the "condo," as he oddly called it), and I just had to tell him that I was doing my job and that he needed to butt out. I was very angry with him for awhile.

Over time, I came to understand that he just couldn't fathom what happened, that maybe he wanted to know that I was drunk, or that something specifically was to blame. Often, I felt the target of that blame. He also tried to help, and he asked me several times if I wanted to come live with him when I was in Columbus. I appreciated the offer, yet his house was a split level with many stairs (I was unable or too intimidated to try crawling up and down stairs), and he would have had to lift me up on the toilet, and he or my step mother would have had to bathe me. I just knew, despite his good intentions, that we both would have been uncomfortable.

Later he concentrated on sorting through hundreds of thousands of dollars of medical bills. He hounded Medicaid and wrote many formal letters, with the help of his attorney, to various offices. He would show up at my mom's place with the "Black Box," as I have come to call it, a black plastic storage container full of dozens of folders of financial papers: insurance forms, records of investments, bank statements, bills (in individual files for each service and utility), and copies of very businesslike and often cold emails to Paul. He expressed his frustrations with my financial situation many times, again making me feel guilty. He didn't always appreciate that I couldn't remember, or even comprehend, many of the details. For months after I returned to Durham, he would say that we needed to "discuss business." I told him once how anxious it made me feel. He lessened some, but eventually continued to have these talks with me, with the added clause "I know you don't like to talk about this, but..." Over time, it has waned. More and more, we would have fun together and have interesting conversations, not about my accident or medical bills, or my possible guilt. When I made a Christmas book with personal photographs in art therapy a few years later, I remembered how and why we used to be close. It helped me have more empathy for what he was going through, when he saw his very capable, intelligent, and successful daughter in the state of losing her mind. He felt helpless, and anger was more accessible for him to feel than anguish.

I also sympathize with how much of a pain in the ass Medicaid became. I still received Social Security payments for years after and went through many pessimistic attempts to get myself out of the system. I was on the phone with them, much of the time on hold, for hours. I still feel panic when yet *another* letter comes in the mail, stating that I have to turn in a stack of personal information, I owe thousands of dollars for overpayment, or I may be eligible for payments (after I struggled to *stop* receiving them). I have tried to be responsible, yet at the same time, not let it drive me insane.

I finally added the thick folder of letters from Social Security into the "Black Box," of which I now have custody. After I returned to Durham, I put it away in my closet; I was hoping that out of sight, it might be out of mind. In the process of writing this book, I dug it out and opened it, discovering more about my history and its effects on my Dad. In one folder labeled June 2007 San Francisco, I found two receipts, subway ticket stubs, and hand-written notes; one dated 6/21/07 notes that a Dr. Pitts says most people who recover well start showing it in 1 to 2 weeks, that I "should be making more progress," "her case is 'worrisome'" and in the margin a "who is Dr. Pitts and why is he delivering this horrible news to me?" Most of the notes are bulleted lists about medical and financial details, yet one says " – could be fatal" and "she could still die," because I was susceptible to pneumonia and infections.

I have read that neurosurgeons are usually pessimistic with their predictions about how the patient will respond to surgery, because brain injury and recovery are so individual and also to prevent friends and family from blaming the doctor when results aren't what they hoped (Cassidy, 120). Yet, their negative attitudes still seem harsh. Dad notes that the doctor's tone was very direct and not at all sensitive. He didn't allow Dad to ask questions. Lots of questions were asked and documented by my Dad. My doctors and my family questioned whether I should stay in California or go to North Carolina or Ohio and who would pay. There were also names of lawyers and questions for them and details on the liquidation of my resources that was necessary for me to qualify for Medicaid. Finally, there were emails to Paul about what bills to pay, which again made me feel sad and guilty.

But I am getting ahead of myself. After my skull reconstruction surgery in October 2007, I started teaching an online class, "Photography: Contexts and Illusions," which gave me a specific purpose and tasks to do every day. I learned later that I had taught the class before my accident, and with greater attention, but still I did well enough to interact with students and to get decent student evaluations. Yet, I had no memories of designing it, or 2 other classes earlier that Spring. Dr. John W. Cassidy (2009) discusses many forms of therapy for people with brain injuries. The suggested therapies or coping strategies that I recognize I used (some initiated by practitioners, yet many developed by me) included: teaching online, making lists (grocery, to do, and numbers lists), telling myself I have a specific number of tasks to accomplish, and using my journals to document events, write emails, and remember details. I began to use my already honed skills of adaption to confront new impairments.

Brandee and my friend, Julie, came to visit me in Columbus after my skull reconstruction, and although I was tired a lot during the time and not quite "myself," I enjoyed seeing them. I only remember one specific evening they came to see me, brought me Japanese food, and watched a movie. I fell asleep during it, but that just triggered my memory about "ladies night," the weekly tradition in which the three of us would get together, drink wine, and gossip or watch bad TV. The awareness was bittersweet. When Brandee and Julie came to Columbus, they gave me even a greater sense of what I was missing.

I began, more than ever, to look forward to going home. Paul called me almost every day from work and would tell me how "the kitties" missed me. Finally, my Mom and I planned a trip to Durham. My house, which I had moved into only about nine months before the accident, felt still new and oddly like I had never left. I don't remember many details about the trip, just not wanting to leave. A few weeks later, I came to Durham for a week without my Mom, I saw friends, and spent more quality time with Paul. Returning to Columbus felt like going back to the hospital, yet I knew it was only temporary. Living in Columbus began to feel like prison, and my Mom and I had more conflicts over what I felt was her resistance to my self-sufficiency. My point of reference became Durham, again, and I finally moved back permanently, just before Christmas.

Paul and I got to spend Christmas together at the end of that long, hard year. We rekindled our romance, and I remembered how to be intimate again. I could say it was like riding a bike, although I have never actually ridden a bike! Later in January, I began to teach fulltime online, as I also taught myself. I reread many of the books on my shelves, reminding myself of my interests and knowledge. I reread old journals, reminding myself of personal history and reengaging my use of journaling as self therapy. Soon I decided to start typing my journals, because I was at the computer a lot already and because handwriting still seemed too slow. I also began my first painting since my accident. I rediscovered my painting studio, kept in a corner of our upstairs spare bedroom/band practice room, and I found a small canvas board next to my easel with a sketch of my finger-free hands holding a paint brush (fig. 3). It seemed like the perfect reentry into my identity as an artist and my interests in how and why disabled people represent themselves. As I applied thick brush strokes and decided on colors – my typical pinks, reds, and blues – my recognizable style emerged. I titled the work *Ann's Hands*, and now it hangs on my living room wall.

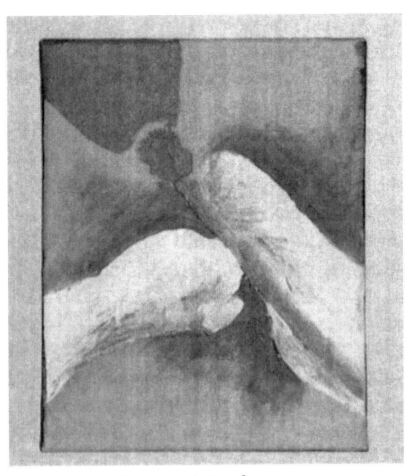

Fig. 3: *Ann's Hands*, 2007

At first, being in Durham made me feel like a character in a science fiction movie, one who had been to another world and was coming home again. Everything seemed new and exciting! I had begun to associate my time in Columbus with only recovering, and my identity had become "the injured patient." Even though I had a lot of fun with my Mom, I craved independence – just to eat something other than cereal in the morning (which I also had eaten in the hospital) and to perform daily activities without being watched. I loved being able to slice my own fruit, program my DVR, and read or write when I couldn't sleep at night. I was slow to feel comfortable going places on my scooter or going out with friends, but once I forced myself, everything seemed like an exhilarating adventure. Whereas I had existed on milkshakes in Columbus, I could now eat my beloved soft serve yogurt cones. They tasted sweeter. And I recall my glee during my first trip to a mall by myself! I could do exercise routines that did not involved therapy practices. I could ignore emails from my Dad about Medicaid, rather than trying to find an excuse to change the subject when we talked face-to-face. I rediscovered many dimensions of myself that glittered between my nagging layers of anxiety.

Everything old seemed new again, and I resumed all my favorite solitary and self-indulgent acts. Yet I also relished spending time with others. My friend Elizabeth visited and took me to the Nasher Art Museum. I had other visitors come see me, and I went out to lunch with Brandee and Julie. Although I would often fall asleep midway through, I began to host ladies night again. I realized I could drink wine, because I was no longer on heavy medication. I definitely had strong emotional moods, and even had a panic attack, in which my heart raced and I just felt unsafe in every way in my own home. Thankfully, I was able to talk to Paul, take a sleeping pill to calm down, and it has never happened since. For the most part, my experiences after returning to Durham were exciting, or quite relaxingly pleasant. Brandee came over one day and planted flowers in my front yard, which still bloom every year. Like the flowers, I was blossoming and committed to moving forward.

I also resolved to pursue everything I ever wanted. Before my accident, Paul and had talked about getting married. We lived and owned a house together, but so far, marriage had only been talk. I suppose I was waiting for him to propose, as was the tradition. If there was one lesson I learned from my experiences, it was that life can be short, and I should never put anything off that I wanted to do. And I knew I wanted to be married and to be married to Paul. Then on a drastically early Sunday morning in Winter of 2008, while butt-scooting on the treadmill, I was watching reruns of "Sex & the City" when Miranda proposed to Steve, and then in hit me. Paul was the perfect man for me because he wasn't intimidated by my go-getting nature, so I decided I would propose to him. As luck would have it, that day I had plans to meet two married couples at the mall for a movie. I told Paul to drop me off early, and I shopped for men's rings. I found one at JC Penney I thought he would like, a slender gold band surrounded on each side with silver, carved bands, so I bought it and managed to hold in my news until after the movie. I think I sat the entire way through "No Country for Old Men" (Ethan and Joel Cohen, dirs., 2007) with a huge grin on my face, which is funny to me because of how dark and gruesome that movie is. After the movie, I announced it to my friends, who wished me luck. Jamie, Brandee's husband, and I joked about how convenient it was that getting down on one knee was my default position! Everyone had no doubts that Paul would say yes, and he didn't even hesitate.

The wedding planning was hectic, but would have been so even if I wasn't suffering from constant sleep deprivation and anxiety. Yet, it was fun, especially once I just decided what I wanted and pursued it. Paul and I aren't exactly traditional, and we wanted that reflected in our ceremony. We considered going to the justice of the peace, but then family members became disappointed, and we gave in and invited immediate family and close friends. Jamie and Brandee suggested holding the wedding at their house, on the backyard deck. I picked out flowers and found a minister online. I tried on dresses, but then found one online that I knew was the one. It was knee length, strapless, and covered in three-dimensional white fabric roses. I also found a vintage wedding hat, which stylishly covered my still very short, almost punk rock haircut (my head had been shaved for my surgery six months earlier). Brandee and Julie, my bridesmaids who both happened to be pregnant, found matching maternity dresses with a floral pattern of my favorite colors: pink, darker pink, and more pink. I put together a wedding mix for the iPod, with nothing cheesy, and helped Paul choose a tux at a vintage store. We were all ready and exited by the time the day came, which was really less than three months since that fateful morning on the treadmill. I didn't see the need to put it off. The ceremony was laid back, yet lively, as everyone celebrated.

Our reception was a fajita buffet at our favorite restaurant, Torero's, and everyone was merry. Paul and I often ate at that location, where they now just bring us our favorite drinks without asking. The other location of that restaurant was the site of our first date. We still laugh about that date. I knew instantly he was a possible match for me when he brought me bottles of wine. Paul knew I was the woman for him when I took him to Torero's and he "ate himself to the bed" (he ate so much he had to lie down after). We have both learned what to order at the restaurant, enjoy activities, and share a bed in even the worst of conditions. I had always known I wanted to be married, and in a twisted way, my accident inspired it. My accident was at first a tragedy, yet brought many people together.

Many memoirs about accidents and other causes of brain injury express the roles of social and family support. For example, the acclaimed book *In an Instant: A Family's Journey of Love and Healing* (2009) is a collaborative project by Bob Woodruff, an ABC news correspondent who was caught in bombing and gunfire while in Iraq, and his wife, Lee Woodruff. The narrative discusses his brain injury and recovery, yet it also describes the history of the couple's romance, their family, and the many supportive friends who helped them through their struggles. The Woodruffs have since started the Bob Woodruff Family Fund Organization: (www.bobwoodrufffamilyfund.org), which provides information and resources for brain injured soldiers and, significantly, their families.

Lee Woodruff has also contributed uniquely to this agenda in her writing; for example, she wrote the introduction to Cassidy's *Mindstorms: The Complete Guide for Families Living with Traumatic Brain Injury* (2009), which serves as manual for families that experience brain injury and which stresses the importance of the role of caretaker or larger support systems. Cassidy attempts to present medical and technical information, as well as resources, in terms that are accessible for the layperson. He states: "When one member of a family sustains a brain injury, the treatment and rehabilitative process inevitably becomes a family affair (12)." In a section titled "Family First," Cassidy explains how and why brain-injured individuals with a support system tend to have lower rates of depression, learn more effective problem-solving skills, and cope better with reentry into their communities. However, some of the common side effects of brain injury can weaken community and family bonds, such as aggressive behavior, sexual dysfunction, and depression. In fact, studies show that 50% of marriages and partnerships end after the first 2 years after brain injury (100). Cassidy emphasizes that strong relationships help reduce these side effects and that feedback from family and friends is most helpful in charting how certain therapy and rehabilitation strategies have worked and in what areas a person needs more therapy. In addition to aiding in the practical challenges of living with a brain injury, support systems help an individual with brain injury to rediscover their identity. Cassidy states: "Family and friends are vital for reestablishing the individual's sense of self" (160). Finally, Cassidy underscores throughout his book that hope is vital.

Hope, I would say, is most beneficial when it comes from inside the one with brain injury and also surrounds her. Like brain injury itself, hope is a family and community issue. I opened this chapter with a quote from *In an Instant*, in which Lee Woodruff explains the many forms of therapy her husband participated in during his lengthy, yet hope-filled recovery. Family and the reassurance of touch highlight the positive influence of loved ones and support systems. She also mentions exercise and music, which are strategies that I have employed and will discuss in the following chapters. Throughout this book, I discuss the power of hope, especially when recovery seems to take a step back.

Brain Injury Moments

"Moment by moment, our right mind creates a master collage of what this moment in time looks like, sounds like, tastes like, smells like, and feels like."
-   Jill Bolte Taylor (2009, 29)

This quote is drawn from neurologist Jill Bolte Taylor's memoir (2009) about having a stroke and echoes with my theme of the many connections between my brain injury and collage. My thought processes and memories specifically are fragmented and often random, and thus, collage-like. Loss of memory has been one of the major effects of my accident, rather than loss of speech and reading or executive functioning skills, which are also common effects of brain injury. Regaining memories of people, places, things, and most profoundly, of myself, has been both fascinating and frightening.

I at first noticed that I forgot people's names and their relationship to me, couldn't picture my home in Durham or how I spent my days there, and didn't have a sense of the passage of time. When I returned to Durham, and still today, Paul will remind me what I want to order in restaurants. I will have sudden flashbacks about people, movies, books, and pieces of clothing, which I find exciting to rediscover, but sad to have lost. One day, I had the image of Meryl Streep in my head, sitting in a wheelchair. Over the next few days, more details would emerge, like the presence of Renée Zellweger and Streep's character having cancer. Then I woke up one morning and thought "One True Thing!" (Carl Franklin, dir., 1988), which was a movie I had enjoyed and was thrilled to watch again. I would see reruns on TV, or shows that I felt I had seen before, but had no idea if I saw it within the last month, or within the past few years. I continue to have memory flashbacks and have no idea where the events or people featured in them factor into a timeline; often these memories are so visually detailed and vivid that they seemed to have happened recently.

In the film "Memento," (Christopher Nolan, dir., 2000) which my brain surgeon recommended that I watch, the main character has had a brain injury that prevents him from making new memories, or has destroyed his short term memory. The film questions the nature of memory itself and suggests how memory is always selective, subjective, and partial. Most poignantly for me, the main character says memory is an interpretation, not a fact. I have noticed how, like memory, memory loss can be selective. I would read my journals, receive emails, or find other remnants about aspects of my life that I am glad to have forgotten – periods of confusion or stagnation, unfulfilling relationships, jobs I wanted and didn't get, and other missed opportunities I pursued. I know I have strategically erased my memory of the accident for self-protection, and I often wonder why certain memories have come back to me while others have vanished. Dr. John W. Cassidy, a neuropsychiatrist who works primarily with patients with brain injury, explains different types of memory loss in the book *Mindstorms: The Complete Guide for Families Living with Traumatic Brain Injury* (2009). Cassidy explains how damage to the temporal lobes, as well as to the hippocampus, affects memory. After reading this research, I believe my episodic (the remembering of series of events), rather than my semantic memory (textbook learning) was affected. Also, my retrograde (remembering events in the past) was more affected than my continuous (remembering of events each day) memory. I can remember random details and events from my childhood, yet I will not remember a place I have been often. I will plan major projects and find out I have already done them, and I won't remember what I ate for dinner the day before. These memory gaps and revelations have become a collage of my "brain injury moments."

Indeed, memory loss proves to be one of the most recognizable results of my injury. Neuropsychologist Rudie Coetzer (2010) also writes that the hippocampus, which is involved in emotion, in addition to memory, is particularly vulnerable to traumatic brain injury. Coetzer discusses in greater detail how memory loss contributes to many subjects' loss of their sense of awareness, existence, and identity, which leads to anxiety. Coetzer repeats throughout his book that, in addition to memory loss, anxiety and depression are the most common emotional difficulties after traumatic brain injury. However, Coetzer states that it is difficult to assess whether and how the injury itself specifically evokes these disorders. Anxiety and depression may be reactions to the physical and cognitive impairments caused by traumatic brain injury, involving memory and executive functioning. Other common effects of brain injury that may increase anxiety include difficulties in self-monitoring, sleep disturbances, changes in personality, and the experience of trauma from whatever caused the injury. I would add to this list the trauma of hospitalization and recovery.

Indeed it is hard to distinguish whether the initial injury biologically causes anxiety or whether the myriad of possible effects of traumatic brain injury are anxiety provoking. For example, issues of poor concentration and attention, memory loss, and problems with executive control functions can lead to anxiety, and word-finding difficulties greatly impact a subject's ability to communicate and socialize. Coetzer discusses how difficult it is to diagnose brain injury survivors with clinical anxiety and depression, because common effects of traumatic brain injury mirror clinical symptoms. For examples, loss of independence and sense of identity, as well as sleep disturbances and fatigue are common effects of traumatic brain injury, in addition to symptoms of anxiety. More clinical markers of anxiety that arise often in those recovering from brain injury, include panic attacks, physical symptoms, avoidance behavior, and loss of confidence. Finally, perseveration (obsession, or repeating thoughts and behaviors) is common effect of traumatic brain injury and can be mistaken for more clinical obsessive-compulsive disorder (Taylor, 56-57; 113).

I am sure that I had anxiety before my accident, but I don't think it was so prevalent or intense. And I don't believe I have clinical anxiety or obsessive-compulsive disorder, although I do see elements of the almost obsessive need for control of the environment, which Coetzer states is common following traumatic brain injury. I have to have things arranged in certain ways and to have my everyday papers, needed objects, and foods available. Coetzer explains subjects feel a loss of control when experiencing cognitive and physical effects of their traumatic brain injury and therefore may take steps to always feel in control (121). Further, memory impairment, and disturbances in self-awareness may contribute to anxiety and depression (48). Like anxiety, many of the effects of traumatic brain injury are also symptoms of depression, although the subject may not have major depressive disorder. I definitely do not have major depressive disorder, yet I did have some depression prior to my injury. I do experience intensified symptoms of depression now, especially guilt, which is a symptom of both mild and clinical depression (Starkstein and Lischinsky

2002, 105-113). Guilt is an emotion that can consume me and negatively affect my behavior. I will discuss later in this book how I have used art therapy to help deal with guilt and the emotions that were at least intensified, if not directly caused by my accident and the experiences following it.

I opened this chapter with Taylor's quote on collage from her memoir, *My Stroke of Insight* (2009), in which she suggests how she views the effects of having a stroke on her work as a neurologist and her perceptions of herself and others. At the age of thirty-seven, she was a neurologist studying schizophrenia when she had a sudden stroke in her home, due to a congenital predisposition of which she was unaware. Her richly detailed, introductory chapters chronicle actually experiencing the sensations of the stroke and the colossal task of seeking help, as she struggles to orchestrate her brain functions. After the debilitating stroke and hospitalization, she relearns tasks or undergoes therapies including reading children's books, having to make decisions on multiple choice questions, putting puzzles together, washing dishes, and going to and operating the machinery in the Laundromat. The following chapters explain the anatomy and functions of all brains. She discusses the interactions between left and right brain hemispheres before discussing the specific effects of a stroke in her left hemisphere:

Just opposite to how our right hemisphere thinks in pictures and perceives the big picture of the present moment.....Our left hemisphere language centers use words to describe, define, categorize, and communicate about everything.......One of the jobs of our left hemisphere language centers is to define our *self* by saying "I am.".......Without these cells performing their jobs, you would forget who you are and lose track of your life and your identity (30-31).

Here, Taylor elucidates how the left hemisphere of brain controls language and communication, while the right side controls emotional sensitivity and appropriateness. These hemispheres also control the movements of the body, yet on the opposite sides. I hit the left side of my brain, but due to internal bleeding and swelling, the right side of my skull was removed. I have been told that only bone was removed, yet I wonder where the other brain matter went, and which side of my brain had been most affected. Because the left side of my head was struck, the right side of my body lost mobility, yet my left brain functions such as my verbal, reading, and writing skills are intact, if not improved. As previously discussed, I do have trouble controlling emotions and putting things into perspective. And I sometimes worry that I am socially inappropriate.

Many of my regretful behaviors are perhaps not completely the result of my brain injury, yet I feel they have been amplified since my accident. An online tutorial offered by the BIANC (Brain Injury Association of North Carolina)[i] states that the following are common behavior effects of brain injury: inability to control emotions, social inappropriateness, and difficulty with relationships. I have experienced all of these. In another memoir written by a physician about her brain injury and recovery, Dr. Claudia L. Osborne (1998) describes in greater detail the major common behaviors associated with brain injury, one of which is disinhibition, or the tendency to be impulsive, to interrupt others, to go off on tangents, and to say and do socially inappropriate things (234). I do notice myself getting worked up about everyday details and blowing things out of proportion. I often worry that I get impassioned about points that might offend others, and I sometimes regret things I have said and done, or at least the ways in which I said them. I have told my Mom to "butt out," informed my Dad indignantly that I will ask when I want his advice, and cried to my husband about how he never thanks me for things I have done, which makes me feel useless and selfishly dependent on him. Over time I have learned to acknowledge these regrets to myself and to others and strive not only to make amends, but to forgive myself.

Osborne's (1998) and Taylor's (2009) memoirs resonate with the medical details of my accident, but more poignantly, they articulate philosophies of recovery to which I aspire. Specifically, their recoveries are also revivals.

Osborne describes how she attunes herself with right brain thoughts and minimizes left brain demands. Many of her actions sound meditative, but most significantly, she learns which brain functions are most beneficial for the kind of person and doctor she wishes to be. Taylor describes consciously deciding which characteristics of each side of her brain to strengthen and which aspects to let go of. Her stroke is a physical blow, as well as an act that leads to insight that, like Osborne's, leads to professional and personal enlightenment. These doctors and writers have made masterpieces from their accidents.

Taylor further articulates her own agency in her recovery and subsequent insights: "Making the decision to recover was a difficult, complicated, and cognitive choice for me" (84). She played an active and conscious role in her healing. I am most proud of the fact that as soon as I knew who and where I was, as soon as I had some consciousness, I knew I would get better. From everything I have read and heard, brain injury is very individual and recovery is unpredictable. The expectations are based largely on who the person was before their accident, such that a person will more likely make a strong recovery if they were already in good physical shape, were physically and mentally active, were driven and successful, and if they had strong family and social support systems. I believe I may have qualified as someone who would have a good chance, and I was told by everyone how remarkably I progressed. I was an over-achiever, an adventurer, and very active; in fact, in San Francisco, a nurse told my parents that I had the blood work of an athlete. Yet, I also think I was successful because I was already disabled; I already knew how to teach myself to do things, and I was very adaptable. I knew how to cope with impairments. My mom says one time we were talking about my speedy recovery, and I said "I have a very strong brain."

In gathering medical records to write this book, I looked at dozens of scans of my strong brain. I saw CT (Computed Tomography) and MRI (Magnetic Resonance Imaging) scans. These are common instruments used for assessing the nature and severity of traumatic brain injury. To my untrained eye, I saw no damage in these images, or anything I would even associate with a brain. The images were not diagnostic to me, but visually fascinating. I printed some on paper and painted watercolor on top of them (Fig. 4).

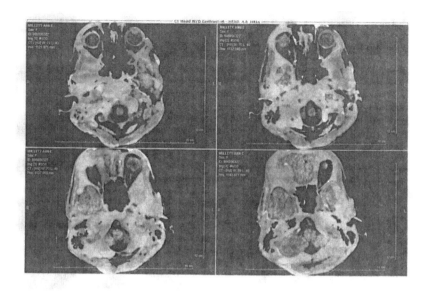

Fig. 4: *Oceanic MRI,* 2011

This four panel image of my brain from a CT scan looked to me like some organic forms. I painted around the dark swirls with blues and greens to create an almost marine feel, as if the images were oceanic forms. I see no brain damage here, just life.

In another more arresting image, I saw a scan of my skull. Here I can see that part of the upper right side of my head is missing. This scan also highlighted the implant teeth I have in my mouth, which makes the image look almost ghostly, like a horror movie skeleton. I attempted to calm the image with my favorite color – pink – but it didn't seem to have any pacifying effect (fig. 5). Here, I see myself in pain and fear, although I was likely unconscious when the image was taken. I am glad that I don't remember any of these details.

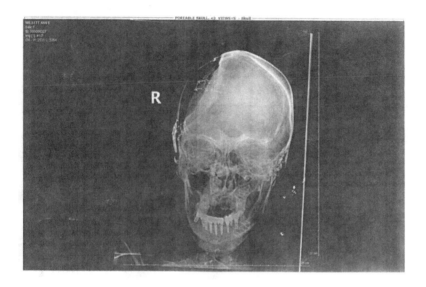

Fig. 5: *Pink Skull*, 2011

I was released from rehabilitation at Dodd Hall at the end of the summer of 2007 and had my skull reconstruction in October. I was told I would feel so much better, so much more together, after my brain was given more space. I was oddly looking forward to brain surgery, but like everything else in the process, and it wasn't without trauma. I can remember lying on my back in the hospital when a man came to put in my IV. My face was covered in some sort of semi-transparent plastic, and I just saw shadows and forms as the physician's assistant tried repeatedly to put the needle in my chest. It hurt, and I cried out, feeling like I was a victim. I must have passed out or otherwise been put out, because I woke up later in a hospital bed with tubes coming out of each set of ribs. The physician's assistant had punctured my lungs, and I had to wait a few days, with tubes coming out of my sides, before I had the actual surgery. I heard later that my neurosurgeon, Dr. Sarkar, was livid.

Dr. Sarkar chose to reconstruct my skull synthetically rather than use my bone, which had been sitting in storage for months, because he believed it was more durable and that he could get better aesthetic results. Rather than the more common procedure of making a plastic mold of the skull piece based on CT scan, he used a fluid form of plastic that hardened as reactants were added to it. The procedure was quite sculptural, as Dr. Sarkar took on the role of an artist. He had started college as an art history major, he told me later, and was quite interested in my art historical knowledge, as well as my art, examples of which now hang in his office. The results of my brain reconstruction were aesthetically amazing, as I now have only a scar that is mostly covered by my hair, as well as functionally amazing. I had been told I would feel much better after the surgery, and although Dr. Sarkar was pleased with the results, he had no medical explanation for this phenomenon. I don't remember anything immediately after the surgery, but I did have more energy and gradually began to recognize that I had a stronger and stronger sense of *being* again. I was much more cognizant. I recognized and related to others and to myself better, as if the world surrounding me before had been abstracted, and now details came into focus. I was not happy with my shaved head, but I wore a wig sometimes and revisited my love of wearing decorative headbands and hats.

In chapter 3, I will discuss the many physical effects of my accident and my subsequent therapies. But first, I would like to explore further the cognitive and emotional repercussions. My intellectual recovery began with teaching a class online and with intense studying of all my books. I rediscovered ideas, made new connections between them, and began to write, with new ambition. Also in chapter 3, I will explain in more detail how I published my first book in the Summer of 2010. I began to publicize my book in the 2010-2011 school year by attending conferences and agreeing to give lectures about my book at universities. I was excited to feel more esteemed as a scholar, yet despite my success, my constant anxiety flared up. I would sometimes feel total panic and nervousness, yet not about anything tangible, and I would project these feelings onto smaller obsessions. I had to have the right dress; I had to make sure I had travel versions of all my toiletries; I needed to remember to save everything to a thumb drive and make multiple copies, just so nothing unexpected to disrupt my precarious feeling of control.

Ever since my accident, I feel everything so strongly, and apparently this is a common result of brain injury. Osborne (1998) defines "flooding" as a prominent effect:

> Flooding: Overwhelmed by, or awash in, one's emotions. This can take place even though the flooded individual does not appear upset or distraught or even consciously aware of being under emotional overload. In a flood, thought-processing slows, and thinking, language skills, and actions may be severely impaired. Flooding may be triggered by external events – the need to make a decision or immediately solve a problem; or from internal pressure – the awareness of one's own confusion, a sense of helplessness, the pain of one's loss of self (234).

Following my accident, I have definitely experienced flooding, by becoming overwhelmed by activities and responsibilities (some of which I needlessly create for myself). Throughout journals I remarked about feeling sad or being constantly anxious and in a hurry. I would worry uncontrollably. For example, when I could not hear him snoring, I would check on Paul to make sure he was still breathing, and I once cried because he came home late, because I was sure he had been in an accident. I became very doomsday! On the other hand, I believe I became less inhibited in ways that benefited me, as I relentlessly pursued my dreams (of getting married, of publishing a book, of making significant artwork). In the process, I also felt guilty for being so self-absorbed. I know I had ups and downs before the accident, but now they seemed more extreme and unpredictable. I obsessed over minute details and established tight schedules for all my daily activities. Since I don't have a clear picture of what I was like before the accident, it is hard to decipher what behaviors are because of it; yet, I sense that every fear, disappointment, and neurotic tendency that might have existed within me before became intensely amplified. I became entirely dependent on sleeping pills and battled often unexplainable fits of anger, resentment, depression, and defensiveness. I began to see how I was constantly judging, even grading myself on how well I performed every action and responsibility. .

I subsequently became consumed by self-scrutiny. Viewing my actions and emotions under a microscope, I didn't always know what I was looking at, and when details came into focus, I often wouldn't like what I saw. My loss of memories made me feel distanced from my past and some of the people in it. I battled constant terror that I would again "mess up," as I blamed myself and often drowned in guilt. I felt guilty about the accident (Was I tipsy? Was I too tired? Was I not paying attention?), about my medical bills, about having to be taken to appointments all the time, and about a thousand little things that helped give me specific situations to project these abstract feelings upon. I can't say my feelings of guilt are all behind me, but it is something I acknowledge more and more. I have learned to recognize my guilt and not let it be a primary motivating factor in making decisions. Accepting responsibility, for me, meant both rewarding my efforts and handing down my own verdict. Further, I battled with my own sense of agency – the ability to make things happen in my life – versus self-blame for my misfortunes. It has been pointed out to me that in my writing and public speaking on this book, I refer to "my accident," rather than "the accident," which, for me, symbolizes how I have internalized it. On the flip side, I also experienced moments of elation and gratitude not only to be alive, but thriving. I didn't know all this was what I was feeling at first and have been able to express it more over time in words, and also in images.

While researching the effects of brain injury in order to write this book, I began to relive them. I was very anxious and hyper, not sleeping well, over-exercising (for two or more hours a day), feeling anxious about going out, and having crazy sleeping (more often, not sleeping) schedules. I felt flooded when I would have many things to do and bored after I rushed though them all. I felt guilt then, for being idle, or for not putting enough time into projects. I even started feeling antisocial, like I felt when I lived in Ohio. While finishing up this chapter, I thought of how I could represent these actions and emotions in an artwork and again returned to collage.

I looked around my desk and in my purse to collect visual symbols of my sometimes frantic state of mind. Because of my memory loss, I am surrounded and consumed by my lists: grocery lists, to do lists, questions to ask people, information to look up online – and the lists go on! I found in my little steno pad, where I make most of my lists, pages of facts, numbers, and names that I obviously thought were important enough to write down and save, but I don't remember why. I also gathered notes written on memo pads and ones that were colorfully shaped like elephants and framed by the illustration of a blue cat. I have multiple notepads on which to make my many lists! I laughed at the little things I would actually write down, like "pillow?," on an elephant-shaped note, which was meant to remind me to check out the neck pillows I saw last week at the grocery store. There are also appointment reminders, lists of artists and movies friends had suggested to me, and notes I made while trying to remember the name of a film I slowly began to recall ("Ruby in Paradise," Victor Nunez, dir.,1993). If I hadn't written these thoughts down at the time they came to me, I would have forgotten them. I also included fortune cookie messages I had kept in my purse, especially one that clairvoyantly stated "You are a lover of words. Someday you should write a book." Like this intuitive fortune, these lists present suggestive, yet incomplete fragments of my thoughts and activities. Assembled in a collage, this barrage of notes to myself represent the chaos that I sometimes feel is my life, here composed ironically by fragments of the lists I make to try to keep myself organized (fig. 6). I assembled all these fragments on a larger sheet of white paper pulled from a sketchbook, and I left the torn edges at the top to match the torn edges of lists in the collage. The collage itself is a sort of master list, or a list of lists. In the center is a list I made the day I was inspired to make the collage, which includes items such as "work on collage," "check weather," and most humorously "make more lists?" I titled this collage *Flooded* (2012).

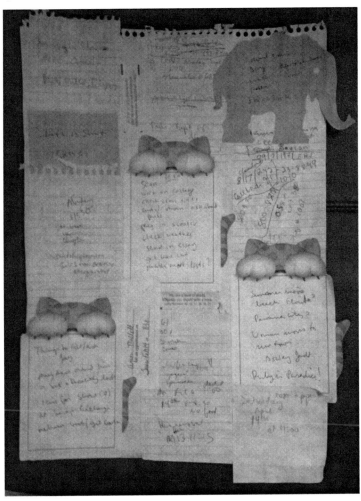

Fig. 6: *Flooded*, 2012

Visualizing my experiences with sensory and emotional overload, this collage reminds me of the work of artist Joseph Grigely. Grigely has been deaf since age 10 and explores in his artwork his phenomenological experiences with the world as a deaf person.[ii] Also a professor of language and literature, Grigely conveys his unique linguistic and social perceptions from communicating with others through silence, shrewd observation of expressions and body language, and written notes. His work explores the connections between spoken and written language. In a series of installations titled *Conversations*, Grigely arranges on gallery walls pieces of recorded dialogue that hearing people have written on paper for him in a range of social situations. The specific kinds of interactions he has and the relationships he shares with the individuals whom he quotes remain strategically concealed, and often these fragmented snippets of conversation are quite random, ironic, and humorous. Grigely's conversation pieces emphasize the fragmentary nature of contemporary communication, as well as his fragmented experiences with verbal communication in a world that does not accommodate those who don't hear.

These and other installations further examine the relationships between the senses and memory, particularly the roles of sound in memory production and psychic retrieval, as well as in forgetting. For example, the installation *Remembering is a Difficult Job, But Someone Has to Do It* (2005) centers on the artist's fragmented memories of the television show "Gilligan's Island," which becomes as a joyful representation of his childhood. Clips of the show's introduction and unforgettable jingle are displayed and heard throughout the gallery, alongside photographs of ocean scenes that become theatrical backdrops, film stills, and imagined visions of a fictive paradise. The work addresses Grigely's memory of hearing and experiencing the show before his deafness, linking the work to his memories of life prior to a childhood accident (as a consequence of which he lost his hearing). Grigely's work represents the role of loss in memory by visually portraying the phenomenological experiences of hearing loss.

Remembering is a Difficult Job, But Someone Has to Do It (2005) reminds me that memory loss is real for and affects everyone, especially as they age, yet that mine might be acute. In works, such as *Conversations*, in which Grigely gathers notes and images drawn on paper, the pieces of paper may vary in size and subject, but are assembled in grid forms that create a square or rectangle composition. Grigely brings order to the disorder. However, in *Flooded* (2012), my notes and lists overlap, obscure one another, and cannot be contained by a frame, as different pieces from notepads spill over the edges of the paper on which they are assembled.

Grigely's work also represents, for me, how loss can open up the possibilities of discovery and enhancement of perceptions. Grigely's hearing loss has fueled his artistic production and perhaps, in some ways, refined his visual skills. My memory loss has likewise fueled my artistic creations and at least altered my perceptions. Michael Paul Mason (2009) discusses the many ways brains can adapt to damage. Neurons can make new connections and the brain can essentially rewire itself, such that the brain has high level of plasticity (169). Mason is a case manager who writes touching portraits or case studies of some of his most memorable clients. Though Mason's case studies vary greatly in types and causes of brain damage, as well as their unique effects and needs, he underscores the role of rehabilitation and importance of receiving funded services. Healthcare reform is needed. Although technologies have improved for diagnosing and monitoring brain injuries, funding and services has drastically declined. I am quite grateful for and indebted to those medical and therapeutic services I have received and would advocate that every victim of brain injury should have access to the same. I will discuss such therapies in more detail in the following chapters.

A Leg to Stand On

Idioms:
a leg to stand on *Slang*
A justifiable or logical basis for defense; support: He doesn't have a leg to stand on in this debate.[iii]

My physical healing progressed along with my social and emotional recovery, but again, not in a linear fashion. In Spring 2008, I saw a doctor in the Physical Medicine and Rehabilitation Department (PM&R) at the UNC at Chapel Hill Hospital. At first I was warm to her, because I liked female doctors, and she seemed laid back. Over time, however, she seemed too laid back, as I felt like she just gave me new drugs or referred me elsewhere. She ended up being another example of why I felt dissatisfied by many medical professionals. But I am getting ahead of myself. She did write me a key prescription for physical therapy, which would greatly help me improve my stamina, mobility, and attitudes about healthcare professionals. I searched online for therapy that could be near my house, because Paul could only drive me on the weekends, and I didn't want to have to ask Brandee to take me to more appointments. I found and emailed a facility called "Triangle Therapy," whose address was potentially in my neighborhood. I hoped that I could ride my scooter there (with my helmet, always!). It turned out that the address was in my neighborhood, and it was the home of a woman who ran a therapy practice. She put me in touch with a physical therapist who did contract work with her (Abby), but who worked largely in Raleigh. I talked to Abby on the phone, felt immediately comfortable with her, and agreed she would start coming to my home to work with me. I loved how she always referred to me as her "client," not her "patient." Now I would hope she would call me her friend.

My physical therapy would come to benefit me in many and sometimes unpredictable ways. Abby came over once a week or every other week and taught me exercises to strengthen my muscles and to increase the range of motion in my hip and knee. Because I had hit my left side of the brain, the right side of my body had much muscle tightness, or contraction. In the hospital, my right arm was bent and held tightly at my side, such that I lost range of motion in my arm and back, and my right knee was at full, unbent extension. We worked on exercises to retrain my muscles to turn on and off at the appropriate times, or in more technical terms, we practice neuromuscular re-education. When we first met, my knee could only bend at five degrees, and over the next few months, I reached about thirty degrees. I practiced bending it with my leg straight and when it was bent at the hip. I also did specific stretches to make my back muscles more symmetrical. As mentioned in Chapter 1, I wore a splint while living in Columbus, which was painful but eventually straightened out my right arm. When I could not move my right arm much, the muscles weakened and caused my back to "wing," meaning that the muscles that held my shoulder blade to my rib cage were weakened so that my shoulder blade "winged" out on my back when I raised my arm. Abby says she could at first put her finger between the underside of my shoulder blade and my rib cage, and that this could have put me at risk for shoulder injuries or pain in the long run. I began to do exercises to increase the strength of my back muscles, such as lying on my back and "punching" the ceiling. Over time, I achieved symmetry.

Abby's techniques inspired my own exercise programs. To increase flexibility and endurance, she introduced me to a Bosu balance trainer, which has become my stage for weight lifting, and she showed me yoga-inspired stretches. In my watercolor *Cripercise* (2009) (fig. 7), I painted myself in fluid strokes of red, orange, and yellow, balancing on my side on the blue Bosu with my arms and legs dynamically outstretched, in a pose Abby had recommended.

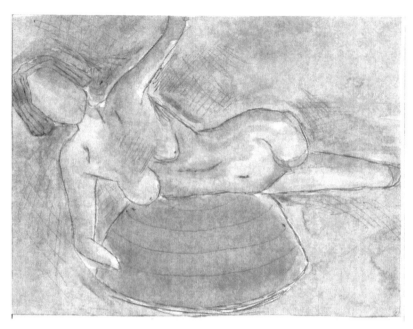

Fig. 7: *Cripercise*, 2009

The disabled body in art has been strategically compared to Classical, and often fragmented forms. In research for my first book, *The Disabled Body in Contemporary Art* (2010), I studied the performance and body art of amputee women who likened their forms to Classical beauties, such as the armless Venus de Milo.[iv] I wished to make similar allusions in my artwork to Classical male beauties, which were traditionally athletes. I called the work *Cripercise* to repossess the once negative term "Cripple" and to designate my routines as a form of exercise specific to the disabled body. Today, the term "Crip" signifies a disability identity that transcends, or perhaps escapes, traditional binaries of disabled/non-disabled or "normal."[v] Further, "Crip" is a designation of pride. In this work, I represent my disabled body as colorful, graceful, empowered, and physically active, contrary to more conventional representations and stereotypes of disabled bodies. Cross hatching lines made with pen surround the body, creating visual movement against the watercolor background. These lines also cross my chest, which could signify that I embody this movement, or perhaps they represent tension in the chest that is released through my actions. On my Bosu trainer, with the instruction from Abby, I performed all kinds of poses and actions.

Abby really was my personal trainer, as physical therapy had been a form of exercise throughout my life. Because I was told at a young age by my doctor, Ernie Johnson, to stay active, I took gymnastics classes and did a lot of swimming as a child. In my *Re-Membering* collage, I included a photograph of myself at about age 8, displaying an active, energetic pose, with arms thrust out and a large smile on my face, modeling a snazzy striped leotard (fig. 8).

Fig. 8: Photograph of Ann Millett-Gallant in Gymnastics
Class, c. 1983

Physical therapy throughout my life had consisted of many activities. Abby communicated with me as her informed client, always explained things to me thoroughly, and was more and more creative, as she got familiar with my unique anatomy and capabilities. We also shared personal stories, books of interest, and discussions of recommendations for places to eat or movies to see. Abby helped me every step of the way as I was fitted for new prosthetics, which proved to be a long and frustrating process. The lengthy fitting sessions and failed experiments got me irritated and pessimistic, and Abby was my one-woman support system.

My new prosthesis raised many challenges. Since childhood, I had used a suspension system for prosthetic legs, which means that my legs fit into sockets and were held in place by a corset worn around my right thigh and belts that attached and encircled my waist. My new prosthesis consisted of silicone sleeves that were rolled on over my legs and had long metal pins at the ends of them. These pins snapped into holes in the prosthetics. I wore one removable belt to stabilize my left leg, yet otherwise, these prostheses were extensions of my legs and had to be manually removed. I had not walked much with my old legs because they no longer fit and did not work well with my knee. Abby says we were able to get it to bend at about thirty degrees, but I needed full range of motion to walk stably. The new prosthesis not only functioned, with practice on my part, but applied pressure on my knee to bend. Yet, the construction and fitting of these prostheses was long and frustrating. My prosthetist and I would sometimes disagree, and I got impatient that my knowledge of my body and its capabilities was questioned. I also got very incensed when he suggested my thick soled, Dr. Martin sandals may have been to blame, and I exclaimed, "I will not wear orthopedic shoes!" This comment may at first seem shallow, yet I was more exasperated by how he was giving me very traditional or textbook suggestions. We would also disagree with how I should put the legs on and take them off. I was more comfortable experimenting and finding my own methods and working with the insightful and supportive Abby. In a progress report, Abby noted: "Ann is able to don and doff the new leg independently and able to balance wearing a variety of different shoe styles on the foot." Abby says she was impressed by my innovative techniques.

After my legs were completed finally, I immediately celebrated with a new pair of shoes. I found online some British Mary Jane shoes with thick, treaded heels, a pattern with pink and purple circles, and a black cat face on the toes. They were sturdy to walk on and eccentric! They matched perfectly with my new helmet; after seeing the movie "Whip It" (Drew Barrymore, dir., 2009) about a female roller derby team, I decided I needed something more fashionable than my black cycling helmet, so I bought a pink helmet online. I had a new look for my new activities.

I have always enjoyed fashion, personally and academically. I have read many times about how Frida Kahlo wore long and colorful, traditional Mexican Indian dresses to "hide" her leg impairments, and I always wondered why she would wear such eye-catching ensembles if she was trying to remain inconspicuous. In works such as *The Two Fridas* (1939), *My Dress Hangs Here* (1933), *Memoria* (1937), and many others, Kahlo features herself in elaborate costumes that express her cultural and personal identities. Kahlo favored the garments from the Tehuantepec or Isthmus region of Mexico, which were specifically pre-Hispanic and multi-cultural. For example, Tehuana embroidery incorporated designs of China, India, and Guatemala. In her many self-portraits and in everyday live, Kahlo adorned and displayed her body in *hipiles*, or traditional, knee-length embroidered white dresses of the Yucatan peninsula; *huipiles*, or Tehuana embroidered garments, designed to go over the head and be worn as a blouse and often worn with a ruffled or embroidered skirt; and *rebozos*, or shawls. She also painted herself in garments with Communist insignia and in nineteenth century dresses, likely inherited from her mother or grandmother, of haute-couture, French-influenced design. In her paintings and on the stages of her daily life, Kahlo performed her allegiance to pre-Hispanic Mexico, to Communist ideals, and to her heritage. All this and more information about the origin and symbolic meanings of Kahlo's wardrobe can be found in a fascinating and beautifully-illustrated book titled, *Self Portrait in a Velvet Dress: Frida's Wardrobe* (2007),a book which was recommended to me by Abby.[vi]

In Kahlo's paintings, her dresses both adorn and flaunt her body on display. As Rosemarie Garland-Thompson has most prolifically articulated, confrontations with pervasive social stares cause the visibly disabled body to be always already on display (1997; 2000; 2001; 2009). It is how one mediates this stare that leads to its larger social significances. Being stared at is a common experience among disabled people, as exemplified by the anthology of disabled writers' work titled *Staring Back: The Disability Experience from the Inside Out* (1997).[vii] This volume includes selections from nonfiction, fiction, theater, and poetry by disabled authors about the experience of living with a disability. A common thread is discussions about social stigma and stares. The editor, Kenny Fries, explains in his introduction: "Throughout history, people with disabilities have been stared at. Now, here in these pages – in literature of inventive form, at times harrowingly funny, at times provocatively wise – writers with disabilities affirm our lives by putting the world on notice that we are staring back" (1). Staring back is an action, as well as a metaphor for putting oneself out there for the world to see.

In everyday terms, I always figured if people are going to stare at you, give them something fabulous to see! "Retail therapy" became a common term between my mother and me, ever since shopping was one of the only ways she could convince me to leave the house in Columbus, and since my more frequent anxiety and mood swings could be forgotten with a trip to the mall. Also, when I didn't feel like myself, when I didn't want to go out or to see people, I could feel more together by wearing something stylish. I remember meticulously choosing an outfit, and putting on mascara, when I went to my therapy appointments in Columbus. My clothing was like a performance of self-assurance, despite that I felt like I didn't have a leg to stand on (i.e., I felt unsupported and unstable).

My processes of physical recovery were, like my collage, my memory, and my thinking, never linear. I had quite a few setbacks that were terribly discouraging. A few months after I began wearing my new prosthesis, my knee began to hurt. It had always been a bit sore from the prosthesis' pressure on my knee, but the pain became more constant and intense. I went to see my PM&R Doctor at UNC, who had no answers. The prosthetist and even Abby couldn't come to any specific conclusions, but just advised me to take it slow. My knee slowly swelled and began to throb and even spasm. I knew something was wrong! Over the course of several weeks, I had a CT scan, a bone scan, and blood tests. I was high on pain killers all through Thanksgiving weekend, when a lot of family members were in town. My Dad took me to some of those tests, had my back as he warned the doctor about how I was a "hard stick" (challenging for medical professionals to insert a needle into), and bought me a soothing McDonald's ice cream cone afterward.

Early in December, just as I was finishing up with Fall classes, I went for an appointment with my doctor, who informed me that I had been diagnosed with a bone infection. She didn't know why, nor did anyone with whom she consulted, but I went home, turned in final grades, packed a bag, and was back in the hospital. I had called both of my parents with the news and they were concerned. I called my Mom again once I knew when exactly the hospital would have a bed for me. When she didn't answer, I knew she was either on the phone with the hospital administrators or doctors, giving them specific instructions and warnings, or she was on her way to North Carolina. She showed up the next day and was able to sit with me in the hospital and help me go to the bathroom with my IV stand. When I was released from the hospital a few days later, I was assigned a nurse, who came over to show Paul how to give me IV antibiotics once a day. In the hospital, I had a PIC line (peripherally inserted central catheter), or a thin needle, inserted into the right side of my chest, with an IV tube suspended by an IV stand that delivered antibiotics into my blood stream. Although I didn't have to be hooked up all day, I had to eat, work, and bathe without damaging or getting wet my pick line, and I felt shadowed by my IV stand. On a side note, Paul now uses this stand to suspend his unique cocktail drum set when he plays with his band, as he turns something negative into something artistic.

After the six weeks on antibiotics, I expected to be all better. But my limited range of motion in my knee sought revenge against my months of training. In a reverse to my previous problem, I could not *unbend* my knee now at all, and I had more spasms, in which my muscles would contract so tightly that I felt my body painfully squeezing itself. I could do nothing to release the muscles and relieve the agony. One morning, I was bawling and screaming in pain so hard that I just instructed Paul to take me to the hospital.

We tried to go to see my regular doctor, but I was sent to the emergency room. I dreaded having to wait for hours, as was usually the case, but perhaps my teary face and tortured tone of voice helped me to get into an examination room sooner. I was given IV pain killers, which worked temporarily, but eventually I was in so much pain again, and by this time had no energy or endurance for it that I began screaming at nurses passing down the hall, "I need drugs!" I was eventually given morphine, passed out, had another CT scan, and was sent home 8 hours later with stronger Percocet pills and valium. Paul kept it together the whole time, but I knew it was killing him too, to see me suffering so much, being powerless to help, and having to spend a whole day in the emergency room.

I then felt completely disappointed by medical practices. Because my knee would not unbend at all, I could no longer wear the prosthesis I had worked so hard with, not to mention had spent so much money on! On a break from classes, I had a couple of treatments in which Botox was injected into my hip and knee to try to relax the muscles, but it seemed to have little effect. I joked to Abby that having Botox over my Spring Break sounded a lot more glamorous than it was! At least I now had prescription painkillers to ease the pain that felt like the piercing of a needle into my muscles. I then expressed to Abby how much I felt passed around and dissatisfied by my doctors, and she suggested perhaps I could try some alternative therapies. She had met a wonderful man, Tad, who practiced craniosacral therapy, which is a form of massage, or more specifically, muscle manipulation that helps all kinds of physical and muscular impairments. In craniosacral therapy, the body is led through gentle movements that are meant to optimize the body's natural healing processes. I met Tad at his office in Cary, NC. He was calm, pleasant, warm, and caring, and he channeled that energy into my leg as he maneuvered my movement on a table. As we talked about my education and interest in art, he made my leg relax enough to extend fully down on the table. Before this appointment, and unfortunately just a day later, my knee and my hip were again tight and immoveable. But we did talk about ways I might incorporate these techniques into my therapies.

After working more on my own and with Abby, I felt that craniosacral therapy was the only place I had seen any positive, tangible change, yet the therapy really needed to be performed in an intensive series of sessions to show profound, permanent results. Tad introduced me to an OT (Occupational Therapist)/craniosacral therapist in Durham, and I began an intensive routine for the weeks I was on Christmas Break. My Mom came to North Carolina to visit and to take me to as many appointments as possible. She said I just seemed more relaxed in general and noted how even when I had been on break from school before, I would still seem anxious and exhausted. I believe I learned how to meditate in craniosacral therapy. While relaxing music played, my hip, leg, and knee were taken through slow and steady movements that increased their range of motion, but significantly also slowed their muscle spasticity. I remember closing my eyes and visualizing colors and shapes in concert with the music and with my movements. I certainly did feel looser in all ways after the treatments ceased, and Abby continued to work with me on some techniques Tad taught her. He also made me iPod recording of "mood music" that was supposed to loosen up my muscles and a CD graphic video of myself, bending and extending my knee steadily to a stream of pink waves. We laughed about how pink was soothing for me.

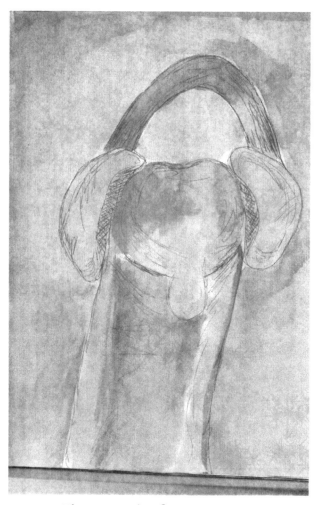

Fig 9: *Music Therapy*, 2010

Inspired by these activities, I made a watercolor and an acrylic painting on canvas, both titled *Music Therapy* (fig. 9). The canvas now hangs next to *Cripercise* in my living room and features the backside of my knee in warm reds, oranges, and pinks, displaying my residual limb, or my "tickle" as I have always called it, and headphones on the sides of the knee. I noticed when I sketched and painted my leg how there was a concave depression at the top of the knee, whereas before my knee cap had created a rounded edge. The composition, from a distance, resembles a face; framed by silver headphones, the backside of my knee and leg look almost like a head and thick neck, as my lighter orange "tickle" resembles a nose. I painted a version of this composition in watercolor in my sketchbook, where I also made images of the anatomy of a knee and of two hands cupped together in the position used in craniosacral therapy practice. I found the forms online with image searches for "craniosacral therapy," and I made my own versions of these representations, symbolizing my newfound interests in and hope for the effectiveness of these techniques.

Craniosacral therapy was very calming for me, but it did not have the profound impact on my knee as I hoped. Spasticity is a common physical effect of brain injury and defined as: "Involuntary increase in muscle tone (energy sent to the muscles from the brain and spinal cord) which causes the muscle to resist being stretched and move in a coordinated fashion."[viii] My knee would be sore and threaten to spasm as I tried to stretch and manipulate it to an unbent position. I still was unable to use my prosthetics, and even more significantly, I was in pain. I finally gave in to what my doctor had recommended, going to a prosthetic clinic to meet with the head of her department and with my prosthetist to discuss how to refit my prosthesis. When she first suggested this, I was not willing to give up; I was not willing to accept that my knee could change so dramatically that I would have to endure the construction and fitting of, much less pay for, a whole new prosthesis. I started to question whether it was worth it.

I had become more used to and at ease with not wearing prostheses. I used to feel never fully dressed without them, and now I felt perfectly socially acceptable and both physically and psychologically comfortable not wearing them. It had been a year since I could wear my prostheses, which I had never been as steady with as before my accident, yet again, I wasn't ready to give up. I did, after all, like having prosthesis for some occasions, liked having another form of exercise, and loved the idea of wearing shoes again! My poor, neglected closet of shoes and dresses was calling for me. Although I had become creative and rather fashionable in stretch pants and elaborate hats, I missed my feminine skirts and fabulous shoes! The doctor at the prosthetic clinic took a look at my x-rays and said immediately and decisively that my joint had fused, my kneecap was dislocated, and that it was not likely that the knee would naturally unbend. After my UNC Doctor's incomplete information and, contrary to my own pessimistic confusion about my body, I was somewhat relieved to finally have a convincing diagnosis.

I began to get fitted for a new prosthesis with cutting edge technology. I would still have the silicone sleeve, but no pin to apply pressure to my knee. I would have a prosthetic knee, and my leg would fit into the prosthesis, with my knee bent, and held on with the suction liner. This fitting and construction process was again frustrating. For example, I was advised to apply a ring of antibacterial gel around the rubber seal of the sock I wore, to help the prosthetic adhere. I thought this was a requirement and was very disarmed when one day it adhered so well that I could not remove the leg, so I crawled to my phone, dragging the leg behind me, and called the prosthetist for advice. I had more experiences getting trapped and needed help removing the limb, until it was better fitted and I learned that using the gel was only a suggestion and not a requirement. I also finally convinced the prosthetist to make the socket of the limb larger when I went to an appointment and challenged him to remove it. I felt a sense of victory when he exclaimed, "Wow, that really is tight!"

After another lengthy series of appointments, I again had legs to stand on. I slowly began walking laps in my house, and eventually made it outside and even around the grocery store with a shopping cart. The knee I have struggled with ever since my accident has taken on all my weight and remains bent, yet strong and functional. I have not, however, returned to wearing my prostheses every time I leave the house, as I used to. They are not totally comfortable and often get in the way. I am proud of how adept and confident I have become in my own skin, which extends around a left leg, or "stump" less than a foot long, and down a right leg, which ends below my knee in my decorative "tickle." I have been able to get in and out of chairs and on and off toilets from my wheelchair or scooter. I have established my own, unique art of mobility.

Standing and walking also caused me additional confrontations with my social identity. For example, when I would go to the store and walk, pushing a cart, I would receive a range of comments with the usual stares. For example, I was told, "You do so good coming to the store, I just wouldn't be able to do it," "How long have you been doing things for yourself?," and "Let me help you." Such "compliments" seem underhanded, as they are based on low expectations of what it means to be disabled. I didn't mind a few questions that seemed genuine, such as when a Kroger employee asked, "How long have you been disabled?" I was impressed that he used the proper vocabulary! I often now wear my Lady Gaga t-shirt that proclaims "Born this Way," so that I am "armed" to respond to the intrusions into my private business. I do however appreciate all the greetings and smiles I receive, because I am memorable and, for the most part, amicable. One time I was wearing perhaps not the most practical, but adorable leopard print flats, when a cashier approached me to tell me I had forgotten an item I had just paid for and, caught off guard, I twisted and began to fall down. He caught me, which I was grateful for, yet deeply embarrassed by. I felt my confidence and agility had been called into question, and I worried that now every time I was in the store, I would be watched with fear and made to feel like I was taking some big risk. Over time, I got over this feeling, and now that cashier is extra nice to me, in a genuine, rather than a pitying manner. While attention is sometimes intrusive and inappropriate, I do enjoy feeing like a local celebrity in my community.

During my struggles with prosthetics and my identity with and without them, I saw a "20/20" news story that captured my attention. It was about Kevin Connolly, who was born without legs and travels around the world taking photographs of people staring at him. He writes in his memoir that he was often stared at in his everyday life, as if he were a tourist attraction, which inspired him to travel around the world to compare the stares.[ix] He notices differences in the types of attention he receives, due to the specific culture which he has entered. Each society reacts to him based on its own cultural values, beliefs, specific histories, and on the status of disabled people in that culture. He decidedly rejected the use and confinement of prosthetics and wheelchairs and instead felt more mobile and comfortable traveling around on a skateboard. His photographs of people, often from a lowered perspective, show the range of facial expressions and reactions his body elicit. Shot all over the world, the photographs frame the stare at disability as universal. They also place the starers on display. The ones staring became the object of the gaze, while Connolly's presence is strongly and illusively alluded to, but remains strategically shielded.

The photographs relate to work I had done in my dissertation and academic papers about photographs of disabled bodies and issues of the gaze/stare. I began to revisit previous research and slowly and methodically constructed an argument about Connolly's work. I felt so accomplished, especially when the paper was accepted for publication in the *Disability Studies Quarterly*.[x] It made me remember how excited I had been about researching and publishing my ideas about disability studies and representation, and I began to think about tackling a goal I had slowly put on the backburner before my accident – getting my dissertation revised and published as a book.

While I was in Columbus, I received in the mail the photograph, *Retablo (New Mexico)*, (2007), by Joel-Peter Witkin, for which I served as a model, just before my accident. Seeing my body featured in the work that had inspired me, hanging on my wall, and reading an article I wrote about Witkin's work that was published in a journal during my recovery made me turn my attention back to an earlier life goal – to publish a book. I got right to work. I had started to attend, but not yet present at the Society of Disability Studies (SDS) conferences, and I renewed my contacts. I emailed people I knew in the field and got recommendations for publishers. I met a lot of dead ends, but then one day in the airport in New York City, following an SDS conference (which Paul now enjoyed attending with me), I ran into an old friend and colleague who remembered and admired my work and told me about his publisher, Palgrave-Macmillan. I inquired with them and through a drawn out and "nail biting" process (I use this term cautiously, as I have never had finger nor toe nails), I finally heard that my book would be published! Again, I felt like my accident may have resulted in a masterpiece in my life, by inspiring me to pursue my dreams.

In this chapter, the phrase "A Leg to Stand On" has signified both my corporeal struggles with my knee and prosthetics, as well as my ongoing battle to feel secure again in my body. "A Leg to Stand On," which I discovered after I began this book, is also the title of a memoir about another accidental masterpiece (1998).[xi] Oliver Sacks, M.D. is a physician and professor of neurology and psychiatry at the Columbia University Medical Center.[xii] He is also a bestselling author who writes case histories of individuals with impairments such as Deafness, Tourette's syndrome, Autism, Parkinson's disease, musical hallucination, epilepsy, phantom limb syndrome, schizophrenia, developmental disabilities, Alzheimer's disease, colorblindness, and migraine headaches. His studies are not two-dimensionally medicalizing, as he highlights his subjects' individuality and extraordinariness. Some of his books include *Awakenings* (1973), *The Man who Mistook his Wife for a Hat* (1985), *An Anthropologist on Mars* (1995), *The Island of the Colorblind* (1997), *Musicophilia: Tales of Music and the Brain* (2007), and *The Mind's Eye* (2010). In A *Leg to Stand On* (1998), Sacks writes about his accidental encounter with a bull on a mountain in Norway and the subsequent damage that was done to his leg. The book narrates his experiences following his accident, such as: he has hallucinations on an ambulance ride; in the hospital, he is heavily medicated and has unfriendly interactions with medical professionals, as well as nightmares; he has fear in the hospital, specifically fear of losing control; he feels disconnected to his paralyzed leg; and he realizes his role has shifted from a doctor (active) to a passive, inactive patient, which he likens to being "a prisoner" (27). I find resonance in Sacks' description of his freedom upon release from the hospital, as well as from the immobility of his knee. Sacks discusses going out after being in the hospital and doing things for himself as being in love with the world. He experiences a sort of rebirth or reawakening of the world and all its simple and wondrous phenomena. He remarks about feeling as though he was visiting from another land are similar to my experiences, described in chapter one, of my return to my pre-accident life in Durham (155).

Sacks' book becomes a meditation on body image and identity. His accident changes, or I would say, decisively improves how he views patients/clients and how he conceptualizes the study of the mind: "We need a neurology which could escape from the rigid dualism of mind/body, the rigid physicalist notions of algorithm and template, a neurology that could match the richness and density of experience, its sense of music, its personality, its ever-changing flow of experience, of history, of becoming" (191). Sacks' accident affected his interactions with patients, as he paid closer attention to their needs and roles as individuals. He discovers the importance of embodied, personal experience, which I wish all medical professionals and any studies of the mind would embrace. My accident, like Sacks', has changed my perceptions of myself, my surroundings, and the abilities of the mind. Sacks also discovered and began practicing music therapy, which I have experienced for my knee. However, my strongest connection here is my own work with art therapy, to which Sacks' music therapy would relate. Throughout this book, I have included examples of my artwork that illustrate my experiences, but perhaps more importantly, they also materialize my perceptions of my body's therapies and changes. Like Sacks' music therapy, I also used art personally as a therapeutic practice, yet I also began to see an art therapist and learned how art can be psychologically and physically healing.

Art Therapy and Collage

Barbara first discovered collage one day as she was working on a drawing that was very technical. 'The center of the drawing got screwed up, so I cut it out and pasted a photo of clouds and sky in the middle. I was blown away by it! That's how I started to collage – **it began as an accident**. That's what collage is, in a way, accidental and surprising."
- Whiting (2008, 2)

In 2008, I assembled the collage about my accident, *Re-Membering*, which I felt was therapeutic and has evolved into this memoir. At the time, I felt intuitively that collage was the optimal medium, since my feelings and memories were already fragmented and existed in diverse remnants of visual culture – photographs, drawings, and get well cards. All these visual fragments that composed my collage, as I discussed in my introduction, composed chains of meaning; one part related to the next and to the next, yet they all lacked one single, central narrative. My consciousness, in many ways, felt like a collage, and visual art gave me a medium to channel my confusion and disparate, sometimes desperate emotions.

Throughout my experiences and throughout this book, I have used my own painting, watercolor, and collage to show images of healing. This practice became more concrete to me in 2009, when I began working with an art therapist, Ilene. These sessions and my homework practices have changed my life and especially my perceptions of my accident and recovery. With my anxiety and explainable mood swings, I felt like some psychological counseling might do me some good, so I explored the options online. I thought it would be nice to have a neutral person to talk to, someone who was not already emotionally involved. I also feared talking through my experiences and feelings, as if it might be painful to rehash my moments of weakness, but I decided to try out art therapy. It was something I was intellectually interested in, and I had confidence about my knowledge of and experiences in making art. I could enter into art therapy with an established sense of expertise. I would, however, discover I had a lot to learn.

At my first art therapy appointment, I filled out a form about my experiences with art and what I hoped to gain from art therapy. The first work I made was a pastel sketch of my cats, a large, orange tabby and a smaller grey tabby, "Sunny" and "Snitty." I then drew myself beside them as an upright, blossoming flower. I also drew a whirlpool, or tornado design above the flower. I talked with Ilene about how I was the flower, and I was spewing out all my frustration and guilt. I often made images and talked with Ilene about my struggles to contain my feelings, and about how my emotions and guilt often overwhelmed me. I felt a lot of guilt from and was offered unsolicited advice from my parents, and I made drawings that portrayed visual boundaries that I felt had to be made. I made many sketches and collages that explored the dynamics of interpersonal relations, with my parents, my extended family, and my friends. These works helped me to visualize my relationships and changes in my emotions.

Art therapy projects also helped me purge my anxiety. I would make scribble sketches, which released my nervous energy. I often built collages around these scribbles with fragments from a box of magazine clippings and with a variety of media, such as watercolor, colored pencil, chalk pastels, and marker. I began to slow down and to try to focus more on the process of my art therapy projects, rather than on the finished project. I strived to embrace art as a way to pause and to appreciate the process. Art making became meditative, as I read about and attempted to practice mindfulness, or the acknowledgement of all the senses and sensual stimuli from the world around me. As I became more aware of my surroundings, I also paid more attention to the patterns of my feelings and behaviors. Becoming more self-aware enabled me to slowly give up the need to control everything, as I felt more capable of anticipating and coping with my feelings. Ilene has said she offered me less directive assignments, as compared with many clients, because I was more verbal than most and my art had its own ways of evolving. Because I would talk a lot, she would sometimes suggest a project or idea as a way of accessing a different part of my brain.

Art therapy projects also importantly marked occasions and the passage of time. I created projects such as birthday cards for myself that would comment on my accomplishments from the past year and express my desires and goals for the year ahead. I also made works about holidays such as Christmas, which specifically visualized that, despite the many conventional activities and expectations that arise at holidays, I had my own unique rituals for celebrating. These projects helped jar my memories of past events and to create a visual record of the passage of time, a concept I struggled with. They also let me see my physical and emotional progress.

The practice of art therapy developed from the theories and practices of diverse professionals. In *Art Therapy Sourcebook*, Cathy A. Malchiodi (2006) states that art therapy developed in the 1970s, although art making has been a part of healing rituals since ancient times. Art therapy is derived from ideas across many cultures that art is a form of communication, it can express emotions and ideas that words cannot, and art helps people understand who they are. Art therapist Judith Rubin (1999) adds that art therapy offers a release of tension, a freedom from the disciplines of traditional talk therapy, and an opportunity to give visible form to forbidden or repressed thoughts and feelings.

Images and creativity are important components in psychoanalysis, in the works, for example, of Sigmund Freud and Carl Jung. Both theorists drew relationships between images and the psyche, personality, emotions, and desire. Psychoanalysis also studied dreams and visual symbols to access the unconscious in the early twentieth century, as Western art work became more abstract to express in visual form the inner world. Many Psychiatrists began to collect the artwork of their patients, as art became a tool for both assessment and psychotherapeutic treatment.

Margaret Nauremburg and Edith Kramer were pioneers in the field of art therapy in the US, exploring aspects of symbolic speech (looking at visual images as symbolic, like dreams) and sublimation (integrating conflicting feelings into visual forms). Nauremburg was also a pioneer in education and worked largely with children. The development of art therapy was related to cultural interests and to developments in education broadly and art education more specifically. Nauremburg was interested more in therapeutic effects of art making and art as a form of communication, whereas Kramer was known more for her writing and theories. Kramer was more interested in sublimation, or making the unconscious conscious and visible. Other prominent figures in early art therapy include Elinor Ulman and Bernard Levy, who helped in establishing the first journal, *Bulletin of Art Therapy*. In the 1930s, the Menninger Clinic in Houston, TX, one of most sophisticated psychiatric healing centers in the world, began incorporating art therapy. In 1968, Mayra Levick started the first graduate program at Hahnemann Medical College, and shortly after, the American Art Therapy Association was formed.

Rubin (1999) further explains how art therapy is helpful for providing a space to express and synthesize a variety of emotions or experiences, such as different times and spaces in an individual's life. Integration is the goal of much psychotherapy, and art therapy offers a means to envision such synthesis. Conscious and unconscious symbols or images can appear in the same work, much like a collage. Further, Malchiodi explains that collage is a popular medium for art therapy, because it appeals to people who may not have art-making experience and may be intimidated by drawing and painting (2006, 92).

I wasn't necessarily daunted by other forms of art, yet collage appealed me because it felt most improvisational. Collage, and art therapy in general, was forgiving. In therapy, I had to let go of the idea that art was pre-planned and intentional. I would sketch images or designs automatically in direct response to Ilene's prompts, and then we would talk through what might have been some symbolic content. I began to open up to Ilene through articulating and imaging my emotions, especially guilt. Ilene discussed the difference between or the interactions between agency and responsibility, or guilt. It was empowering to feel like I have agency, like my actions cause events or successes to happen, yet I began to understand that I can't take responsibility for every misfortune. I felt relief when Ilene questioned my stubborn assumptions and told me that all the countless things I felt guilty about were okay, such as cancelling plans when I felt too overwhelmed. I needed some permission for my feelings and doubts, as well as a way to materialize my own forgiveness. One day in September 2009, when I was talking about my guilt over the accident, and how defensive and anxious I became when my Dad brought up that he "still didn't know what happened," Ilene enthusiastically suggested writing a forgiveness letter. I dictated and she recorded:

> To Ann (written to self in the third person)
> It doesn't do yourself or anyone else any good to belabor why. There are no answers to these questions. Like Mom says, you may be more careful & more cautious these days and that is a good thing. To feel guilty all the time is not going to help you or everyone that loves you. You succeed in so many ways, in so many parts of your life. You have lived because your life is important to yourself and to other people. You have learned so many things in this accident that made your life better and that made you

closer to people in your life. How much you mean to the people in your life. You mean so much to the people around you. Your relationships have gotten stronger and that is a positive thing. Let go of the guilt, stop letting the guilt hold you, control you, hold you back.
P.S It wasn't your fault
P.S.S. Look forward

I would often feel frustrated by having guilt or anxiety or depression, especially when I could not attribute these feelings to anything tangible in my daily life. Emotions would seem to erupt from nowhere or were unexplainably intense. I would tell Ilene how I would try to meditate or make art at home or otherwise distract myself, but that sometimes, nothing seemed to work.

In December 2010, I vented to Ilene that I was a doer, and I just don't know what to do to make myself feel better when I didn't understand what I was feeling in the first place. She then asked me if I had been eating and sleeping all right, which was related to a larger question about whether I was depressed. Then she said that I had been through great trauma, that depression and anxiety were the clinical effects, and that maybe now that my prominent medical issues were resolved, these feelings were setting in or just more recognizable. I pointed out that when I was having issues with my knee and my legs, at least I had something tangible to attribute these feelings to. The whole discussion was interesting, and at the very least, it made me feel less guilty about having anxiety and depression.

In addition to helping me question my guilt, art therapy has helped me explore memory loss and to regain memories. In December 2010, Ilene suggested an art therapy project of making my own children's book, or rewriting and redesigning an old favorite. I was also telling her that I had been realizing that my memory loss might be affecting me more than I had realized, because I don't have a lot of memory of my emotions, or I don't feel very connected to my history. I don't remember how I felt in certain situations, and I don't have a lot of nostalgia; for example, I don't remember how Christmas made me feel in the past (It was December, and I was surrounded by "Christmas.") Memory loss related to the book project, too, as Ilene suggested that I take a children's Christmas book and rewrite and reimage it to suit my own history of and feelings about Christmas. I tried to think of an appropriate book to work with, but then I just decided to work from scratch, or in other words, work from the remnants of memory available to me. I searched through a large tub of old photographs I had found in my closet, scanned and printed ones from Christmases past, and wrote captions for each one. This exercise not only helped me to recall past Christmases, but it also rejuvenated some of the feelings I had toward family members.

For a specific example, I printed a copy of a photograph of me as a young child, wearing red Christmas pajamas, seated on my dad's lap as he reads me a book (fig. 10). We are in the living room in the house I grew up in, seated beside our family Christmas tree. I wrote the following caption:

> We spent a lot of time in the living room of the house during the Christmas season, in front of the fireplace and beside the Christmas tree. I am sitting here on the lap of my dad, Steve, while he reads me a story. I was always Daddy's little girl.
> He was a very attentive father, and I looked up to him. In many ways, professionally, I have followed in his footsteps. It seems like now he makes me anxious and defensive so often, that I feel sad.
> And guilty.

Fig. 10: from *Ann's Christmas Book*, 2010

Ann's Christmas Book gave me a good project for Winter break and made me feel a sense of nostalgia about Christmas. This picture and caption made me remember why I had once felt close to, and even idolized my Dad. It also helped ease some of the strain I had recently felt between us. That Christmas day, I called my Dad and we gossiped about our holiday activities and the people present at them. We also talked about seeing the movie "True Grit" (Joel and Ethan Cohen, dirs, 2010) together when he came to Durham later that week. I feel like making my Christmas book had made me change some of my recent feelings about him and calmed my defensiveness. The Christmas book, like many of my art therapy experiences, was healing and helped me regain some of what I had lost.

Throughout my recovery, I had worked on art projects, as discussed in Chapter 3, which helped me renegotiate my body image. Specifically that Christmas, art therapy images helped materialize my faith that craniosacral therapy could be the magic cure for my unexplainably tense knee. Ilene said to me in art therapy that I seemed to have a sharp sense of the interactions between mind and body. I was so flattered! While I was lamenting my pain and frustration over my knee, Ilene suggested that I create a healing image. I thought for a moment, picked up a pink marker, and drew a circular, spiral design. I explain that this was healing for me because it was my favorite color and because it represented for me movement and a dynamic release from my muscle contraction. I returned to this image again and again in art therapy projects, especially collages, as the spiral reappeared. I realized that one of my favorite necklace pendants was a white, blue, and green spiral. I was especially astonished when, doing internet image searches for craniosacral therapy, I would find spiral designs used to symbolize craniosacral therapy. It seemed very clairvoyant!

Upon further research about art therapy, I learned that circles and *mandalas* (or "sacred circles") were forms specific to art therapy, because historically they been associated with sacred forms of the universe and cosmology. Malchiodi (2006) explains: "While a mandala drawing will not magically reduce anxiety and troubling emotions, studies have shown that drawing within a circular format...can have calming physiological effects on the body in terms of heart rate and body temperature (127)." My pink spiral, which I began to relate to a mandala image, would have healing affects psychologically and corporeally.

The mandala also has history specific to the ancestry of art therapy. Psychoanalyst Carl Jung (2000) used mandalas in his theories and practices. Jung related the mandala shape to the universe and to the layers of the psyche, and he believed that working with mandalas helped individuals achieve "individuation," or discovery of the true self. Jung states: "The symbol of the mandala has exactly this meaning of a holy place, a tenemos, to protect the center. And it is a symbol which is one of the most important motifs in the objectification of unconscious images. It is a means of protecting the center of the personality from being drawn out and from being influenced from outside" (150). Jung believed that the mandala image was protective and potentially effective. Jung was a psychoanalyst who originally studied with Freud and followed in Freud's theories about how a person's history and unconscious could affect their conscious actions. However, Jung believed people could change their unconscious neurosis, especially through creative acts. He coined the term "active imagination" to characterize the significance of dream images and fantasy; for Jung, the images created through active imagination, or through art therapy, brought unconscious thoughts and images to the awareness of the conscious mind, such that the images and symbols that emerge through creative play help to merge the conscious with the unconscious. Jung's term "creative play" specifically signified artistic acts that are meditative rather than focused on the final product, such as the acts practiced today in art therapy. The mandala, for Jung, was a therapeutic symbol as well as a tool that suggest the wholeness of self. Dream, fantasy, and mandala images specifically, created spontaneously or unconsciously, were insightful and healing. The act of creating these images was important, yet so was coming to terms with them, or considering and discussing their significance with a therapist. Jung practiced an early form of art therapy on his clients, as well as for himself.[xiii]

Ruth Berry's book on Jung (2000) summarizes the main tenets of Jung's work, which, for me, resonate with the medium of collage. Jung advocated the unconscious and often spontaneous association of images, such as in the construction of collage, as a healing practice. As previously discussed, collage is often used in art therapy for people who may feel intimidated by or uncomfortable with making other, more traditional art forms. Yet, upon closer examination, collage also embodies a history of containing personal and political commentary. Art historically, the medium of collage mixes abstraction and realism, crosses two-dimensional and three-dimensional genres, and incorporates performance, improvisation, and found objects. Collage crosses and challenges the differentiation between and statuses of high and low arts, of arts and craft, and gendered materials and practices.

Collage has historically been associated with avant-garde art movements and practices. Surrounding the Soviet revolution and World War I, the art movements of Dada and Surrealism paraded practices of anarchy and parody, specifically through engaging different genres of visual culture, as well as performance and poetry. Surrealism especially celebrated illogical, automatic associations and dream imagery, following Freud's emphasis on symbols and images as representative of feeling and desire. Such challenges to the status of the arts were challenges to the status of authority and to social status. Collages specifically championed political movements, such as Communism and Fascism. Cubist and Constructivist collages in the first half of the twentieth century embraced the images and practices of the working-class, specifically rejecting the products of the bourgeoisie. Specific examples of Cubist collage, such as Picasso's works, challenged the traditional visual perspectives and styles of Western art and mixed Western with non-Western forms. Following World War II, the influential Peggy Guggenheim supported collage in New York, which was now filled with European artists in exile. While Abstract Expressionist artists such as Jackson Pollock incorporated paint, paper, and other scraps in his Surrealist-inspired, spontaneous attacks on his canvas, sculptors of this time period, such as Robert Rauschenberg, created three dimensional sculptures of collaged found objects to again challenge the status of high art. Many artists also attacked the post-war rise of commercial culture through collage. Pop artists, such as Andy Warhol and Roy Lichtenstein, critiqued the commerce surrounding "high" art by incorporating practices of silk screening, commercial printing and other forms of popular culture, such as comic books, into their museum and gallery-worthy collages. In this vein, the idea of "collage" could extend to later twentieth century assemblages, happenings, and the formations of a Queer aesthetic. Finally, a form of collage called photomontage combines photographs drawn from documentary, family collections, entertainment, and advertising, often combined with typographic fragments, to question and confuse the aesthetics and conventions of these genres and to question the role of the photographer. The designation and form of Collage has expanded as the world of visual culture expanded.

Collage has also played a prominent role in the visual history of the Civil and Feminist Rights movements. In his collage *Prevalence of Ritual: Mysteries* (1964), Romare Bearden explored the status of Black artist. Bearden's collage shows the richness of African-American cultural and visual history, by including magazine images he was surrounded by growing up in a rural working class family in North Carolina, as well as by referencing African-American folk traditions, such as collecting, quilting, and jazz music, and it also contains elements of African figurative sculpture. The collaged pieces compose a series of figurative images drawn from popular culture (such as a stereotypical "Mammy") to photographs of Civil Rights leaders, showing the range of identities and three dimensional experiences of African Americans. Throughout the collage are images of trains, signifying communities of people who live near trains and also to physical and spiritual travel.

In addition to the politics of race, collage has embodied the Feminist movement, specifically by engaging the high art forms that were traditionally a masculine domain with traditional "women's work," or crafts. *The Dinner Party* (1974-79) was a multi-dimensional collage-like project, or installation, crafted by hundreds of women and some men led by artist Judy Chicago. It contains nine hundred ninety nine notable women's names written on the floor, surrounded by a triangular table of thirty nine place settings, designed specifically to honor thirty nine notable women, both mythological and historical, who have been conventionally overlooked by history. *The Dinner Party* was an attempt to rescue women's history and merge domestic labor with creative production; it incorporates clay and ceramics, glass, metal, wood, fibers (in the forms of weaving, textiles, tapestry, and quilting), jade and lacquer, bronze casting, stone carving, ceramic sculpture, and glassblowing. This collage honored specific women, as well as the artistic work of women everywhere, and it stands prominently in the Feminist Art movement.

While this has been an admittedly rushed and partial history of the collage, I have presented these examples to begin to elucidate how collage, as a medium, has historically symbolized a disruption of the status quo. Bringing together visual images from disparate contexts also initiates the process Jung prescribed for bringing one's unconscious thoughts and desires to visual, material, and conscious forms. Collage making may also be a form of meditation or an opportunity for catharsis. In *Living Into Art: Journeys Through Collage* (2008) artist Lindsay Whiting profiles members of the Sonoma Collage Studio, formed by artists Audrey von Hawley and Barbara Jacobsen, in which collages are assembled individually and discussed as a group. Whiting discusses how collage frees the maker from left brain analysis to enable right brain creation and how many members see the studio community as an art group, a support group, a therapy group, and a political meeting – all rolled into one (80). For these group members, as for me, collage is intuitive, improvisational, and therapeutic. I opened this chapter with a quote from "Barbara," a member of this collective. She exclaims her discovery (epiphany) that her collage started as an accident, and that collage itself was "accidental and surprising" (2). Collages are, in many ways, accidental masterpieces.

Throughout my work in art therapy, I have filled a number of the pages of my sketchbook with collages. They juxtapose sketches in pencil or pen, images cut from magazines, old watercolors I found in past sketchbooks, and pieces I found in a bag of cards and other remnants that my mother assembled for me throughout my time in San Francisco and Columbus. In the summer of 2010, I assembled a collage of these collages, an arrangement of pages glued to a square canvas, surrounding a central image of my healing pink spiral (fig. 11). Directly below the spiral is a fetishistic collage of shoe images I admired and cut from magazines, representing my desire to be able to wear my prosthesis and new shoes. The shoes I selected were mostly ones I found aesthetically beautiful, and even fanciful, rather than practical. Because I have prosthetic feet, I can only wear shoes with only a slight heel, so I could only dream of wearing the colorful, adorned, and strappy high heels that abound in the collage. Some of the shoes appeal to me as aesthetic, non-functional objects, such as pink heals covered with lace that would surround the foot and climb up over the ankle. In the bottom left corner is a Grecian style silver flat I could imagine being worn by a theatrical goddess, and beside this photograph, is a disembodied black strappy heel, posed with fruit and a wine glass in a still life composition. I could possibly wear the series of flats that descends on the right side of the collage (if I could afford them!), or the rainbow-colored, high top tennis shoe at the top of the collage with wings on each side. These shoes remind me somewhat of my own cat-faced tennis shoes, yet are even more outrageous. This collage to me is about fantasy, retail obsessions, and on a lighter note, humor.

Fig. 11: *Art Therapy*, 2011

Above the central spiral, opposite to the shoe collage, is a collage of women wearing a variety of fashionable costumes. The performers include: a red haired and made up woman modeling a flowing pink gown; an image of a famous portrait of Marie Antoinette, known as both a prominent historical French monarch, as well as a leader of the period bustled dress and high hairdo fashions, seated in her finery with one arm raised; a picture of Lady Gaga from her *Paparazzi* video (2009), standing with crutches; a headless model or mannequin displaying a flowing, layered bridal gown; and a remake of a Man Ray photograph of the woman from behind, showing the poetic lines of her shoulders, back, and rear end. In the lower left corner are more references to fashion, in the form of a pair of shoes and a hand bag, which I cut out of a Thank You card I had received. Eyes pervade the collage, from Marie Antoinette's gaze on the right side, to a closed eye with luscious and long eyelashes at the left, and, predominantly, the top of a woman's head wearing a hot pink wig, jeweled tiara, and heavily made up eyes, which peer over the edge of the bottom frame. Images of eyes fascinate me, for they cause the viewer of the collage to feel like they are both looking and being seen. The composition stares back at me. I also included in this collage of many fashion images a picture of a polka-dotted helmet that I admired. I later bought myself the pink one.

To the right of this collage is another one composed of eyes, looking back, looking away, and not looking outward, but rather, looking inward. I began a sketch of a photograph of Queen Latifah I found in a magazine, and I liked how I rendered her dramatic eyes, looking off to the right, but I somehow got the proportions of her lower face terribly skewed. No matter! I just glued down over Queen Latifah's lower face a watercolor I had done a few years ago of a yellow and green female body, lying on her side with her eyes closed, as if she is asleep. Sleep had been such a struggle for me since my accident, and in this collage, the sleeping figure is protected by a pair of striking eyes pasted above her, Queen Latifah's determined gaze. Also surrounding the sleeping figure is a fantasy image of a model wearing a clingy black dress and black gloves, with her brassy blond hair fanning out around her, and the black and white photograph of a little girl, or maybe even a fairy, dressed and posed like a ballerina, looking back at her audience with pride and hope for approval. I also included in the remaining blank spaces images of shoes and a bouquet of white roses, specifically laid in front of the sleeping figure. Her head is angled towards a small, separate image to the right of this collage, which is a print of an illustration I found online of the anatomy of the knee. I colored it in with bright-colored markers to seem more appealing, although my knee had caused me great pain and frustration and often made it that much harder for me to sleep. Despite that this knee is trying to disrupt this collage, the sleeping figure is at peace, as I aspired to be, with a number of goddesses watching her back.

Directly below this is a less unified, but more concrete collage. I began to just cut images from magazines and catalogs that appealed to me. Often, I would not know why they spoke to me, until I had them speak to each other. I had found in my bag of remnants a card that came with a bouquet of flowers Paul had sent me when I was in

Columbus. It comments on how amazing he thought I was doing when he had visited, and it says "I love you." Paul wasn't someone who often made large romantic gestures, so I was especially touched. I also saved the envelope from the first mailing my mom had sent me after I was married, which was addressed to "Mrs. Ann Millett-Gallant." It materialized my identity now as a married woman, yet perhaps not a terribly traditional one, because I chose to hyphenate my name. I assembled these pieces with random images from magazines, which made compositional and symbolic sense with the card and envelope: a long, thick strip of white flowers that reminds me a wedding décor; a close-up of a diamond ring or bracelet with interlocking knots; a vibrant, colorful painting of pink, yellow, green, and blue vertical stripes; and a small image of cups of red, orange, and yellow paint, with a paintbrush, symbolizing how this collage was an accidental masterpiece.

I assembled these collages in a few different arrangements before I glued them down. I wanted to create visual chains of meaning between them. Below this collage is a photograph of my prostheses while they were in the process of construction, modeling my pink, purple, and black cat, favorite new shoes. The lower half of the right leg is not yet covered with a "skin," but here shows a metal skeleton. When this photo was taken, I was in the process of learning how to walk again and still working with various adjustments to the alignment of the knee and foot. This photograph fits well in the corner created by the edges of my "wedding and such" collage and my collage of shoes. Next to these legs is a design of three spirals, which I colored with green marker. I wanted to repeat the spiral design to draw the viewer's eyes back to the center of the composition. Opposite of this green spiral, which sits in the lower right corner of the larger composition, is a sketch I had made of a wine glass, in pen with blue, purple, and pink watercolor hues, and with a spiral drawn in the circle of the glass's rim. Drinking wine relaxed me and helped calm the jumble of thoughts and to-do's that often overloaded my brain. I placed the sketch at a diagonal, with the spiral aiming towards the center spiral image and the stem of the glass filling in the top left corner of the canvas.

Beneath this wine glass and to the left of the central pink spiral is a light-hearted collage I made of one of my passions, sushi. I collect sushi paraphernalia, and I reveal it here in a photograph of me sitting on my couch, surrounded by my collection of sushi pillows, which Paul has been collecting for me over birthdays and Christmases. I also included a picture of the sushi wall clock which hangs in our living room and an image I found online, which I think is some sort of head wrap. The sushi pattern on the fabric is the same as on a headband I own and often wear when I go out for Japanese food. Finally, somewhat dominating the composition, is an image that caught my attention in a magazine of the word "go," created entirely of colorful sushi rolls. I didn't know what I would ever do with the image when I spotted it, but it all came together when Paul bought me my most recent sushi pillow. This collage represents my fondness for sushi and collection of sushi items. It reveals how humor and play always factor into my collages.

Below this sushi collage is another in a much different tone. The collage, which I call "The Two Anns," features a reprint of the photograph of me which was included in the newspaper when I lived in Columbus and which shows the depression in my skull before it was reconstructed. Part of the newspaper article is included beside the image, with the title "Willpower" and information about my educational history at Ohio State University and the University of North Carolina at Chapel Hill and about my skull reconstruction surgery. This newspaper clipping is in the upper right corner of the page, and to offset it, I glued down in the lower left corner a larger photograph of me that was shot in my hot tub. I model a new, pink, and jeweled bathing suit top, as I hold my flexed arms up to display my much worked for muscles. Behind me, on the edge of the hot tub, is a glass of wine, making the image look like one from a celebration. I see this pairing of images as almost a before and after. Both of them were not very focused and clear when I printed them on my black and white printer, so I emphasized the ethereal quality by painting the background a deep, ocean blue. Black spirals entangle in this water space, wrapping around and visually connecting the two images: one that is somewhat iconic of me in recovery and one of me laughing, posing, and having fun.

The composition is reminiscent of Frida Kahlo's *The Two Fridas* (1939), in which she painted herself twice, once in a European, stiff, white dress, and on the other side, in a Tehuana *huipil*. These images have been likened to Kahlo's split ethnic identity, but also to contrasting sides of her identity in general. Significantly, the figures are holding hands and bound together by veins which spiral out from hearts, which are painted outside of each Frida's chest. Kahlo was influenced by medical illustration, which shows in these hearts, as they bleed through connections that have been cut. These medical illustration objects in Kahlo's composition relate visually to my marker-colored illustration of the anatomy of a knee, which I included to the upper right side of the canvas. Kahlo's painting is, for me, about recognizing and reconciling the opposing sides of her heritage and identity. I am continuously trying to reconcile my identity as the victim of an accident and as a patient, with the aspects of my personality that are more joyful.

The composition of all these images on canvas, which I titled *Art Therapy* (2010), is a larger attempt to draw connections between the dimensions of my identity and personality, before and after my accident. They represent my experiences as colorful, multidimensional, and varied. The composition also documents my work specifically with art therapy and with collage. I filled the canvas as much as possible with a variety of images and painted any remaining surface in the same pink shade as the spiral. All the diverse aspects and experiences of this time period in my life surround this dynamic and expansive, hopeful image of the spiral. They also rest upon a soothing and appealing shade (at least for me) of pink. This work was composed over many months and from different stages of my experience, and the process of putting these pieces together as an aesthetic compilation was meditative. Writing about this collage helps me to understand exactly why it is therapeutic.

Art can be therapeutic within and beyond one's work with an art therapist. Professional artists have attested to the psychological benefits of making their work. For example, in her memoir, *Infinity Net: The Autobiography of Yayoi Kusama* (2010), the Japanese born artist states that her work was therapy that treated her "psychosomatic illness":

> Born into a hopeless situation with parents who did not get along; growing up tossed about by the daily storms that raged between mother and father; tormented by obsessive anxiety and fears that led to visual and auditory hallucinations; asthma, and then arrhythmia, tachycardia, and the illusion of "alternative bouts of high and low blood pressure" and

"blood seeming to flood from the brain one day and drain from it the next"; such eruptions of mental and nervous disorder, wrung from the scars left on my heart during the hopeless darkness of my adolescence, are fundamentally what keeps me creating art.[xiv]

Kusama here describes her unhappy childhood, in particular her absent and philandering father, her overbearing and explosive mother, and her physical and psychological disorders. Art helped her deal with her threatening visions and hallucinations and her intense anxieties, and she states that her art was a replacement for psychiatry. Kusama is best known for her New York exhibitions in the 1960s of paintings with repetitive and hallucinatory dots and installations of boats filled with or furniture covered with sewn and stuffed phallic forms, as well as paintings and sculptures composed of uncooked macaroni. She discusses in her autobiography how these works were not only reflections of, but therapeutic for her obsessive/compulsive disorders, anxieties, complicated relationships, and deep-seated fears. In the late 60s and 70s, Kusama became notorious for Happenings that protested war, politics, capitalism, and most profoundly, sexual repression. Kusama recruited groups to gather in the nude, she states, as a means to deal with her own aversion to sex and gender politics. In her Happenings and work in her studio, models were often covered with her obsessive polka dots, as their bodies became de-individualized and parts of a lager pattern.

Kusama's later literary work continued these trends. She discusses in her memoir about feeling suicidal, and her list of novels includes *Manhattan Suicide Addict* (1978) and *Double Suicide at Cherry Hill* (1989).

Kusama is an extreme example of an artist who clinically needed intervention; however, many artists without such neurosis may use art as a meditative and healing practice. In my first book, in which I analyzed many disabled artists' representations of their disabled bodies, I resisted the idea that their work was necessarily therapeutic: "Disabled artists are unfortunately often disregarded by the mainstream audience or assumed to express images of so-called suffering (like Kahlo) and the desire to be 'normal.' Their work may be seen as acts of overcoming their disabilities and therefore forms of therapy and rehabilitation (2010, 16)." Here, I was resisting the notion that disabled people are always in a state of rehabilitation, as if terming their work as "therapeutic" was placing it in a medical model. Now, I would say the best art, to me, is therapeutic, or cathartic. Kahlo's bold, confrontational, and resplendent work was therapeutic, I believe, for herself and for many viewers and scholars. I suggest that calling art work "therapeutic" doesn't necessarily point to the infirmity of the artist, but rather, to their humanity. After all, who *couldn't* benefit from some therapy?

Forgiving

My experiences with traumatic brain injury and recovery have changed my life in numerous and unpredictable ways. My personality may seem the same to my loved ones, but I believe that I am more anxious and emotional than I was before my accident. I seem to feel everything so strongly, and my mood swings are extreme, erratic, and often without justification. My sleeping is very irregular, and I am dependent on sleeping pills. I can't stay up at night and am often up at two or three in the morning, although the fact that I have always been a morning person, I work from home, and I can make my own schedule play roles in this routine. I am also not as mobile as before, as I do not wear my prostheses as much, have more trouble walking when I do wear them, and I don't drive a car. I always drove with my prostheses (the "normal" way, by using the foot pedals), but I don't know if I ever felt completely safe doing so. Now, if I drove, I would have to use hand controls, and I have considered learning how to do so. Yet the idea of handling such a vehicle and being in traffic scares me too much. I just don't trust my reflexes and worry that I would panic. However, not wearing my prostheses in public has also made me feel more comfortable in my own skin.

The effects of my accident prove negative and positive. If it had never happened, would I be married today, and would I have published my first book? I definitely wouldn't have written this work. To erase this event and its many effects on my life would be to tear down collages, weaken relationships, and change history in all kinds of ways. I remind myself of this often, as I battle my own guilt for my accident and the pain it caused others. Yet, guilt certainly is not productive in showing others my gratitude and in moving forward with my life. No one blames me for my accident except myself. I was watching The Oprah Winfrey show one day in 2011, when she quoted a definition of forgiveness as "giving up the hope that the past could have been any different." I have learned that forgiving myself does not mean that I am sanctioning anything that happened, such as the money and sense of security that were lost, nor does it mean I am disregarding all the pain and regret my accident has caused. Not constantly blaming myself allows me to be more grateful and to take full advantage of my life. Writing this book has played a huge role in my ability to process all these events and to feel all these mixed emotions.

In February of 2012, I was invited to speak on a panel regarding disability and visual arts at the California College of the Arts in San Francisco. I decided to extend the trip a couple of days in order to see some of the sites of my time there in 2007, such as the hospital and the sidewalk in front of the café where my accident occurred. As discussed earlier in this book, I characteristically experienced high levels of anxiety before every trip, especially ones in which I was speaking in public. I often get frustrated that this happens every time, because I would think after experiencing a number of such trips, and having them go relatively smoothly, some of that angst would lessen. Yet, going to San Francisco caused a unique stimulus for anxiety, because of the specific history I was about to face. Although I focused on seeing this history as research for this book, I found myself in anguish and in tears. I started having nightmares about being lost in a strange city while hallucinating and riding on an uncontrollable scooter. I tried to come up with excuses not to go. I was afraid I would be unstable through the whole trip and vowed that if I was miserable the entire weekend, I would no longer make such commitments.

The weekend was actually very nice. Paul and I stayed in the hotel where he had stayed with my mom while I was in the hospital. I had heard that he walked a lot on a trail surrounding the San Francisco Bay, and this time, I accompanied him and saw the hilarious diving ducks he had told me about. This time, we shared a fascination with them. On our first full day in San Francisco, Paul and I drove by the hospital and the site of the accident. It was somewhat sad, but more anti-climactic. I was impressed by how Paul was giving me a tour of the neighborhood surrounding the hospital, with its magnificent houses, extreme hills, and panoramic views of downtown. It felt strange that I was the reason he was here in the first place, yet I seem so absent in his stories about San Francisco. Maybe it was therapeutic for him to see it all again, and this time, to have me by his side. When we drove past the café where I tipped the scooter off the curb, I again felt guilt. I was hoping to see that it was a precarious setting, as my mom had claimed. It looked like a typical curb next to the street, rather than the unguarded and steep drop off I had imagined. She has told me that she could tell exactly how the accident had happened when she visited the site. Then that guilt passed, as I tried to just let go of the obsession to know what went wrong. The only conclusion I can come to is that there was a constellation of events, none of which could be predicted, that caused me to lose control of the scooter and tip into the street. I felt and articulated to Paul that it was time to move on.

Writing this book has helped me come to terms with my experiences and to continue to move forward. It began with an essay I wrote, in response to my own assignment, for a class I was teaching called "Art of Life" in October 2008. The class explores through readings and examples the intersections between daily life and art, how to view life as an art form, and the unexpected masterpieces that arise from accidents. The students are asked to write a series of four essays which combine visual and critical analysis with personal narrative. One of these essays is about loss or being lost and how loss leads to new insight, discovery, and artistic creation. In response to this assignment, I posted an essay to the class website for all the students to read, which has become the introduction to this book. I thought I would set a good example by completing an assignment myself, but I didn't anticipate the effects this would have on my students and on my class. I received a number of compliments on my writing and admiration for my strength and determination. I also received anecdotes from students about relevant experiences they or their loved ones had been through. I believe sharing my history and struggles with my students makes them trust me more, encourages their honesty, and helps them produce poignant and insightful writing.

Over time, I began to see how my personal writing could affect many individuals. The memoir has been a prolific genre of disability studies literature, expressing disability as an embodied perspective on life and as subject position. The 2004 publication, *Traumatic Brain Injury in the United States: Emergency Department Visits, Hospitalizations, and Deaths*, published by the Centers for Disease Control and Prevention (CDC), reported that 1.4 million Americans sustain a traumatic brain injury every year and 80,000 to 90, 000 of those individuals experience permanent disability as a result.[xv] More recent statistics report that more than 1.6 million people suffer from traumatic brain injury every year,[xvi] and that brain injury may be one of the most prevalent and tragic consequences of the Iraq War.[xvii] I wrote this book for individuals with brain injury and their friends and families, as well as for a broader audience of readers interested in art, art therapy, and disability studies. I also wrote it for my own friends and family, as well as myself.

List of Figures

All works, except photographs, by Ann Millett-Gallant

Fig.1: Photograph of Ann Millett-Gallant in the San Francisco General Hospital, May/June 2007

Fig. 2: *Self-Portrait with Hemicraniectomy*, 2011

Fig. 3: *Ann's Hands*, 2007

Fig. 4: *Oceanic MRI*, 2011

Fig. 5: *Pink Skull*, 2011

Fig. 6 *Flooded*, 2012

Fig. 7: *Cripercise*, 2009

Fig. 8: Photograph of Ann Millett-Gallant in Gymnastics Class, c. 1983

Fig 9: *Music Therapy*, 2010

Fig. 10: from *Ann's Christmas Book*, 2010

Fig. 11: *Art Therapy*, 2011

All images may be viewed in color at:
www.facebook.com/remembering.millett.gallant

Endnotes

---

[i] See: http://www.nctbitraining.org/. This informational course was developed by Project STAR at Carolinas Rehabilitation and is supported in part by Health Resources and Service Administration (HRSA) Traumatic Brain Injury Implementation, Grant #H21MC06746, Contract Number 1906-09, from the North Carolina Department of Health and Human Services, Division of Mental Health, Developmental Disabilities and Substance Abuse Services (DMH/DD/SAS), and TBI Project STAR at Carolinas Rehabilitation.

[ii] Images of Grigely's installations are available online at: http://www.gandy-gallery.com/exhib/joseph_grigely/exhib_joseph_grigely.html; http://web.mit.edu/lvac/www/exhibitions/FALL/1996/conversations.html; http://www.gandy-gallery.com/exhib/joseph_grigely2/exhib_joseph_grigely2.html

[iii] I draw this definition by the Idioms section of The Free Dictionary: http://idioms.thefreedictionary.com/have+a+leg+to+stand+on

[iv] Millett-Gallant, Ann. *The Disabled Body in Contemporary Art*. New York: Palgrave-Macmillan, 2010.

[v] See, for examples, McRuer, Robert. *Crip Theory: Cultural Signs of Queerness and Disability*. New York: New York University Press, 2006 and Sandahl, Carrie. "Queering the Crip or Cripping the Queer?: Intersections of Queer and Crip Identities in Solo Autobiographical Performance," in *GLQ: A Journal of Lesbian and Gay Studies* 9, n1-2, 2003, 25-56.

[vi] Olmedo, Carlos Phillips , Denise Rosenzweig, Magdalena Rosenzweig, Teresa del Conde, and Marta Turok, *Self Portrait in a Velvet Dress: Frida's Wardrobe. Fashion from*

the Museo Frida Kahlo. San Francisco: Chronicle Books, 2007.

vii Fries, Kenny, ed. *Staring Back: The Disability Experience from the Inside Out.* New York: Penguin Putnam, Inc., 1997.

viii I draw this definition from the website of the Brain Injury Association of North Carolina: http://www.bianc.net/

ix Connolly, Kevin Michael. *Double Take: A Memoir.* New York: HarperCollins Publishers, 2009.

xMillett-Gallant, Ann. "Staring Back and Forth: The Photographs of Kevin Connolly," in *Disability Studies Quarterly* 28, n.3, Summer 2008.

xiSacks, Oliver. *A Leg to Stand On.* New York: Summit Books, 1998.

xii For more information about Oliver Sacks and his many works, see: http://www.oliversacks.com/

xiii See Berry (2000) and Jung (1997).

xiv Kusama, Yayoi. *Infinity Net: The Autobiography of Yayoi Kusama.* Chicago: The University of Chicago Press, 2011, 94.

xv See http://www.cdc.gov/

xvi I draw these statistics from Cassidy (2009, 19) and from the website for the Brain Injury Association of North Carolina: http://www.bianc.net/

xvii See Woodruff (2007, 281).

Select Bibliography

Berry, Ruth. *Jung, A Beginner's Guide*. London: Hodder & Staughton, 2000.

Cassidy, John W., MD. *Mindstorms: The Complete Guide for Families Living with Traumatic Brain Injury*. Philadelphia: DA Capo Press, 2009.

Coetzer, Rudie. *Anxiety and Mood Disorders Following Traumatic Brain Injury: Clinical Assessment and Psychotherapy*. London: Karnac Books, 2010.

Jung, Carl. *Jung on Active Imagination*. Princeton, NJ: Princeton University Press, 1997.

Malchiodi, Cathy A. *Art Therapy Sourcebook*. New York: McGraw-Hill, 2006.

Mason, Michael Paul. *Head Cases: Stories of Brain Injury and Its Aftermath*. New York: Farrar, Straus and Giroux, 2009.

Osborn, Claudia L. *Over My Head: A Doctor's Own Story of Head Injury from the Inside Looking Out*. Kansas City: Andrews McMeel Publishing, 1998.

Rubin, Judith Aron. *Art Therapy: An Introduction*. New York: Taylor and Francis, 1999.

Starkstein, Sergio E. and Alicia Lischinsky. "The Phenomenology of Depression After Injury," *NeuroRehabilitation* 17 (2002).

Taylor, Jill Bolte. *My Stroke of Insight: A Brain Scientist's Personal Journey*. New York: Plume Publications, 2009.

Whiting, Lindsay. *Living Into Art: Journeys Through Collage*. Hot Springs, CA: Paper Lantern, 2008.

Woodruff, Lee and Bob. *In an Instant: A Family's Journey of Love and Healing*. New York: Random House, 2007.

CPSIA information can be obtained at www.ICGtesting.com
Printed in the USA
LVOW06s2153050214

372572LV00011B/153/P